TWO COUNTRIES, ONE LIFE

Encounter of Cultures

TWO COUNTRIES, ONE LIFE

Encounter of Cultures

Carlos G. Vallés

GUJARAT SAHITYA PRAKASH
P.B. 70, ANAND - 388001
GUJARAT, INDIA.

The author can be contacted at:
www.carlosvalles.com
carlos@carlosvalles.com

ISBN 973 93 80066 04 2

Price: Rs. 150.00

Cover Design: Elena L. Butrón

Published by K T Mathew, SJ, Gujarat Sahitya Prakash, P.B. 70, Anand –
388001, Gujarat, INDIA.   Printed by Agnelo Vaz, SJ, Anand Press, Anand,
Gujarat.

INDEX

A FOREIGN VISA

This morning I had a little experience which may well open this book. I went to the EMBASSY OF THE P. R. OF CHINA IN SPAIN, CONSULAR SECTION, to apply for a visa. I found the proper counter and I stood at the end of the line. It was a long line. But then a thing struck me at once. Most people, almost all the people in the long queue, were Chinese. Their features, their eyes, their small height, their speech gave them away unmistakeably. They were all Chinese. And they were all young. There was only an old man, with a typical sparse goatee on his chin, who was accompanied by a young girl, but the rest were all young generation people. There were also a couple of Spaniards, to be sure, conspicuous by their loud talk and wide gestures, but they were just a spot in a landscape of Chinese faces. Wasn't that strange?

I would have expected visas to be for tourists or business people, for Spaniards who wanted to see the Great Wall, the Forbidden City, the Tiananmen Square, the Ming Tombs or the Xian Warriors, or maybe to strike business deals with the emerging economy of the Eastern Dragon. But what were all those Chinese people doing in that long queue for visas at the Chinese Embassy? How could a Chinese person be applying for a Chinese visa? Was I standing in the wrong queue?

All were holding ready in their hands their application forms together with their passports. And then the penny dropped. I tried to look unobtrusively to verify my first tentative discovery. Yes, they were all Spanish passports. The passports they all held in their hands were Spanish passports. Those Chinese people were Spanish citizens. Immigrants. People who had left their country for a distant land, had successfully established themselves in their business or their jobs, had fulfilled all the requirements for citizenship in their new country, had applied for it, obtained it, had spent several years already away from home, and wanted now to visit friends and relatives, to preserve links, to keep in touch, to integrate the culture of their past with the surroundings of their present, to strengthen their roots in order to be able to extend their branches, to make sure they could always come back and be accepted in the land of their birth if the day would come when they would like to come back to it for good, to bring their small children, born in Spain, to know the land of their ancestors, of their heritage, of their culture in China. For that they needed a Chinese visa on their Spanish passport. And so they were standing now in the long queue in front of the window for *VISADOS,* which is "visa" in Spanish. The word was, just in case, printed in Chinese characters by the side. The fee was 25 euros. 60 euros for a rush fee with delivery on the same day.

Standing in the queue after the unexpected revelation, I was reminded of an incident in my own past. I was one day talking in Ahmedabad, India, with a revered person and dear friend, Umashankar Joshi. His name is a household name to people of my generation in India. Poet, writer, Vice Chancellor of the Gujarat University, Member of Parliament, founder editor of the monthly magazine *Sanskruti,* a word that means "culture" and which was the reflection of his own personality as culture incarnate, and thoughtful friend who could converse simultaneously with people of different languages who did not understand each other but all felt at home in the presence of the universal host. I had by then been many years in India and was planning a visit to the country of my birth, Spain. He asked me one day at that time about my work and my plans, and I answered him:

- I'm planning to go abroad.
- Do you mean you're going to Spain?
- Yes, I'll be going to Spain shortly.
- And do you notice how you've said it?
- What do you mean?
- Do you notice how matter-of-factly you've pronounced the word "abroad"?
- Well, yes, I suppose so.
- You see, you are a Spaniard, you've been now a number of years in India, have learned the language, have identified with the people, and now that you are going to your own country you say you are going abroad. You don't say you are going "home". You are going "abroad". And you say it so naturally that even you have not noticed it.
- Thanks for telling me. If it was creditable of me to speak thus, it is even more creditable of you to notice it. And to tell me.
- Just think. No Englishman posted for duty in India under the British Raj would have said "I'm going abroad" when he was going back to England on furlough, whatever the number of years he might have been in India.
- Right. For them going to England was always "going home". Well, I guess home for me is now India.
- That's what you've just now spontaneously implied. You said you're going "abroad".

-   I'll soon be back.

His word had touched me. Home. Abroad. I spent 50 years in India, from my 24th in 1949 to my 74th in 1999. Then I came back to Spain. That makes me an immigrant twice over, as I felt as strange when I came back to Spain after 50 years as I had felt in India when I first arrived there. Or, perhaps, and this would be closer to the truth, I felt at home in both places. This is the auspicious approach – as we say in India – to begin a book on immigration.

A MISCHIEVOUS SMILE

I did feel at home in India when I first arrived. I was even surprised at the easiness of that first arrival, as on those days there was hardly any contact between continents, I knew nothing about the East in general or India in particular, words like "globalisation" or "inculturation" had not yet found their way into the dictionary, and the world was not a global village yet. And still, and in spite of the heat and the pungent food and my scanty knowledge of English coupled with my total ignorance of Indian languages, I did feel I was in friendly surroundings, I sensed I was accepted, I felt at home in India from the start. When I mentioned that fact to one of my first Hindu acquaintances, he had a ready explanation for that. He told me (also quite matter-of-factly!) that I felt at home in India because (obviously!) in my previous birth I had been an Indian.

This first incident on Indian soil set me thinking. Reincarnation to me at that moment was a remote concept. For an instant I just nodded and smiled warmly at the stranger and to me a totally foreign suggestion. Rebirth, reincarnation, metempsychosis, or transmigration of souls as it was severally called had been only a one-line corollary in my philosophy textbook at the university in Spain. After dealing extensively with the nature of soul and body and their union in Aristotelian terms, a few conclusions were drawn at the end, and the last one was this single line which I still remember in its concise Latin: *Ergo reiicitur theoria transmigrationis animarum.* "Consequently, the theory of the transmigration of souls stands refuted." And that was that.

Now I was standing before a person to whom "the theory of the transmigration of souls" was as evident as it was absurd to me. That could have led to an argument, to a quarrel, to a knowing smile, to an estrangement..., or to a learning situation. The man in front of me was at least as intelligent, as sensible, as knowledgeable as I was, and he took reincarnation for granted in his view of life and his explanation of many differences and problems of the human existence, while I held the opposite view, and was wholeheartedly convinced that belief in reincarnation created more problems than it solved. And then I reacted. Unconsciously, instinctively, surprisingly, perhaps naively I heard myself saying to my friend who had explained my situation with a reference to reincarnation: "Of course! That must be it. How is it I hadn't thought of it? I must have been an Indian before." And we both smiled.

This does not mean that I became a believer in reincarnation. I did not. But I had learned that we could be friends even while holding different views. More than that, we could learn from each other, we could broaden our mutual views, we could accept the limitations of our convictions and the claims of the other person's convictions, we could understand how a person could live and be happy in their life and consistent in their views while thinking quite differently from what we ourselves where thinking, we could become better friends and richer persons by sharing our points of view with interest, curiosity and respect. We could grow as persons.

I take this incident as an image and a parable of what the encounter of cultures should be. I was not going to argue with my Hindu friend, to try to convince him, to browbeat him, to win him over to my view, to belittle him, to despise him, to defeat him. And, again, I was not going to change my own view, to feel inferior, to cow down, to abandon my own belief in a false attempt at making myself accepted in my new surroundings. But I did learn to live side by side with a person who saw some things in a different way from mine. I had truly and bluntly encountered another culture face to face, and I had benefited by the encounter. I even learned how to use other people's beliefs to their advantage. When later in my teaching career college students would approach me for help not only in their studies but also in their personal problems, I could use as a motivation for moral behaviour the principles I knew made sense to them, and so I would remind a Hindu student how a serious misbehaviour in this life could bring him a low birth in the next, and I knew the teaching would strike home. I was not, thereby, forgoing my own beliefs, but I was using the other person's beliefs to help them on their own terms and with their own language. It would not have helped them if I had tried to impose my own personal motivation on them. To argue them out of their belief in reincarnation would have deprived them of the strongest moral motivation in their tradition. I respected their faith.

A day came when a college student whom I had helped in his mathematics and in his family problems told me spontaneously, "How is it that I feel more affection for you than I feel in my own family? In our previous birth you must have been my father and I was your son; that's why I love you as my father". I was then ready with my reaction and answered with parallel spontaneity, "Yes, and I love you as my son." And we both smiled, though my smile had a slightly different curve from his.

WE ARE ALL EMIGRANTS

Migration began early in human history. The first book of the Bible records a significant one:

> "Since Lot, who was travelling with Abram, also possessed sheep and cattle and tents, the land could not support them while they were together. They had so much livestock that they could not settle in the same district, and quarrels arose between Abram's herdsmen and Lot's.
>
> Abram said to Lot, 'There must be no quarrelling between us, or between my herdsmen and yours; for we are close kinsmen. [Lot was the son of Haran who was Abraham's brother, and so they were uncle and nephew.] The whole country is there in front of you. Let us part company: if you go north, I shall go south; if you go south, I shall go north.' Lot looked around and saw how well watered the whole plain of Jordan was; all the way in Zoar it was like the Garden of the Lord, like the land of Egypt. So Lot chose all the Jordan plain and took the road to the east. They parted company: Abram settled in Canaan, while Lot settled among the cities of the plain." (Genesis 13:5-12)

"The land could not support them" and "quarrels arose". We seem to be reading today's newspaper. People emigrate because of poverty in their countries or because of war between factions. They want to better their prospects or to escape hardship. The problem is that now virgin lands are not easily available and migrants cannot find space "among the cities of the plain". They now reach countries that are already overpopulated and cities that are overcrowded. It is not as simple as saying, "if you go north, I shall go south; and if you go south, I shall go north". Today people come from the South to the North and from the East to the West, only to find the North and the West already full of people who occupy the land and frown at the newcomers. Even when the North needs the South and the West needs the East for labour and growth, the North and the West look with suspicion and mistrust towards the South and the East. The generosity and big-heartedness of Abraham, patron saint of all emigrants, remain sadly forgotten, back in the first book of the Bible.

Abraham was an old hand at migration. His own story had begun when God had unexpectedly called on him and had ordered him out of the blue: "Leave your own country, your kin, and your father's house, and go to a country that I will show you." (Genesis 12:1) To leave one's country and to go to a land yet unknown is the essence of the human adventure which Abraham, father of all peoples, first enacted with courage and faith. This is the destiny of every human being in the development of their life, the change in their ideas, the flourishing of their personality. We all end up by being quite different from what we once were. We all change our views and our behaviour from the time we start thinking under the influence of people around us till we find ourselves in the strength of our own independent personality. Our land, our home, the coordinates of our life map keep changing. We all feel called to another land, at least in thought, in projection, in imagination. We all are children of Abraham, and it is from him that we have inherited the urge to emigrate, to go out, to leave our land, to explore a land that we do not know yet but that "will be shown to us" as we advance in life with joy, with passion, with danger, with courage, with hope. We are all emigrants.

We are all emigrants because, even if we do not change our country of residence, the country itself changes, and those of us who were born in the twentieth century find it already a little strange to live in the twenty-first even if we still live in the same country. Geography has not changed, but mentality, customs, atmosphere, way of life, culture and environment have so much changed all around us that yesterday's films make us laugh, and we already take as history events of our youth, while we speak a language which is quite different from the one young people speak today. We have emigrated from a cultural environment to another in half a century even if we have not changed places, and we know it. We have emigrated to the land of computers, robots, cell phones, outer space, transplants, credit cards, instant news, global mobility. This is another planet and we have not yet quite landed on it.

We have emigrated to distant boundaries, as, formerly, the world was far away in lands and ideas, and now it is at our doorstep. We have changed our environment because our environment has changed for us. Now we are not just members of our club or of our neighbourhood, but of the whole country, of the whole of America and the whole of Europe, of India and China, of Australia and Africa, right up to the islands of the Pacific and the glaciers in the Antarctic. All that has come to our door on screen and films, in tourism and research, in story and image. Every neighbour is Marco Polo, and every friend is Christopher Columbus. Events from the whole world and the whole of creation reach us instantly and shape us as village gossip or city news did before. In our imagination we have emigrated to the frontiers of the cosmos. We are all emigrants because we all live now in surroundings that put us in contact with people of different mentalities, different cultures, different languages, different customs, traditions, religions which we used to consider as alien and remote, while we see them now practiced in our own neighbourhood next door. All around us has changed.

Finally, we are all emigrants because we are destined to a different future. If the first book of the Bible has called us all emigrants, one of the last books reminds us of our permanent status telling us that, "we have here no lasting city, but we are seekers after the city which is to come." (Hebrews 13:14) We are on our way. We are, and will always be, emigrants. If we reach a place, that is only to leave it again for another. Always on the move.

> "They acknowledged themselves to be strangers and aliens without fixed abode on earth. Those who speak in that way show plainly that they are looking for a country of their own. If their thoughts had been with the country they had left, they could have found opportunity to return. Instead, we find them longing for a better country, a heavenly one. That is why God is not ashamed to be called their God; for he has a city ready for them." (Hebrews 11:13-16)

> "Aliens and foreigners." (1 Peter 2:11)

> We are all emigrants.

A LETTER TO GOD

We now live side by side, shoulder to shoulder in the cities of the world. We do rub shoulders but we don't quite mix. Features, colour, accent, dress define identities and mark boundaries. Ghettoes, cantonments, Chinatowns, Latin quarters have existed and continue to exist, though without the name now and without official demarcation. But we all know the zones and identify the dwellers. This grouping offers protection to the new immigrant and can as such be helpful and necessary; but it has the danger of perpetuating separation and preventing integration. We have to keep in mind the hardships of first-generation immigrants to appreciate their courage and to understand the development of succeeding generations. I knew a student in those early days who went from India to the United States with only 5 dollars in his pocket and a telephone number of an Indian friend in America. He spent his 5 dollars managing to call his friend from a public phone at the Kennedy airport in New York on arrival. His friend greeted him warmly... from Los Angeles! He stayed on, worked hard, learned skills, found a job, climbed slowly, and eventually became a highly successful entrepreneur in the textile industry.

Not all cases ended up so well, though. Here is another first-generation case, though more recent in occurrence and more touching in its pathos. The publishing house PPC of Madrid, Spain, on completion of 50 years in the business in 2005, invited fifty persons of different fields to write "a letter to God" in faith and fiction, and all the letters were then published in a volume with the title "50 Letters to God". The writers were ecclesiastics or laypeople, believers or even atheists, philosophers, artists, professional writers and people on the street, and between them they reflected in a personal way the delicate and variegated texture of human relationships with God. One of the letters had been written by a young emigrant from a Latin American country to Spain. This is what he told the Almighty:

> "I'm writing to you, God, though I don't believe much in you, but my mother does, and it is on her account that I am writing this letter to you. I'm writing to ask you the following favour: Please, God, allow my mother to remain in ignorance. Please. Keep on permitting that my mother may not get the money or the papers to come to Spain to visit me. Keep on permitting that she may continue to believe my lies about my doing fine here, my having a good time as she knew I always wanted, my being successful in every way among good people and good things.
>
> I am ashamed, God. It is ten years now, maybe more, since I left my country. I was the fearless adventurer who was going to conquer the world, who was going to get my family out of its poverty. And now... I am a dependant on the benevolence of a state that refuses to accept me as its citizen.
>
> Look here, God, I don't know why you have victimised me. But I accept it. I took the wrong decisions, I let myself be dazzled by the glamour of Europe. OK. But she has done no wrong. She lost a son when I came

away to find fortune in a foreign land, and she revels in her dream-come-true of her son being accepted and respected in the country he has conquered thanks to his intelligence and his drive.

My mother would die if she would see how thin I am and would guess the sicknesses I have suffered. So, please, God, do keep maintaining her ignorance, and keep also maintaining my capacity to lie to her when I call her on the phone, once a month, and I feel transformed, if only for a few minutes, into the winner she wants me and believes me to be. This, at least, you owe me." *(50 cartas a Dios,* PPC, Madrid, 2005, p. 154)

Here is another true story, again one of the many such stories of human suffering across continents.

"Rosaura came from Bolivia to Spain to join her husband who was in the country for two years having found a job in Madrid, and had called her now. She came with her three small children, Natalia (12), Edison (6) and Victor (3). She had mortgaged her small house in Bolivia to pay for the journey. Rosaura is only 30, but looks much older. She is small and swarthy, with dark, almond-shaped eyes, wearing the poncho and the hat of the *cholitas* in the Andes. But she does not smile. The children also look grown up and do not smile. They do not seem to understand what is happening. And their mother cannot explain it to them.

When she arrived at Barajas (Madrid airport) there was nobody waiting for her. She managed to make her way with her three children in tow to the address her husband had given her. When she rung the bell, a strange woman opened the door. Rosaura thought she must be one of the several people who shared a flat, as she knew it was common practice among immigrants, and went in. Her husband came up, and the children rushed to embrace him. When she approached and made to kiss her husband, he drew back. 'This is now my woman, Rosaura', he said while he drew the other woman to himself and held her close at the waist. She was slim and blonde. Rosaura froze, and, shaking, managed to ask him: 'Then why did you make me come all the way here?' He answered coolly: 'To sign our divorce.'

Rosaura, Natalia, Edison, and Victor live now crowded into a small room whose rent is 300 euros a month. Rosaura looks after an old lady who pays her 400 euros a month. Her eyes look smaller each day. Her children avoid company. They are illegal immigrants. Reluctant immigrants." *(Alfa y Omega,* 28.12.06, p. 32)

There are even more traumatic experiences at the fringe of the wide spectrum of emigration, and their existence should be acknowledged with respect and fellow feeling to enlarge our awareness of this problem, wide as the human race and deep as the human heart. Ayaan Hirsi Ali escaped sufferings at the hands of fanatics in Somalia, found refuge in Holland where her first job was translator from Somali to Dutch, and narrates thus her first experiences in her job:

"I bought clothes to go to work as a translator, normal western clothes in place of the veils and kerchiefs and robes I wore in Somalia. A black frock down to my knees, a long shirt tailored to fit, and shoes. My first mission consisted in translating for a Somali man who was asking for asylum before the police. For me it was a momentous occasion. I relived my own experience as a candidate for asylum, only that now, less than three years after, my position had changed. The man gave me the once-over in contempt and asked me: 'Are you the interpreter?' When I said yes, he laughed in mockery and said: 'But you are naked. I want a real interpreter.' I translated his words for the Dutch official, and he said: 'I decide who translates, not you.'

I was only a mechanical cog in the process, as a typist. That thought quietened me. Even though the contempt of the Somali man hurt me, I knew I had to learn to control my feelings if I wanted to be a professional. It was my job, a simple transaction, just like packing cases in a workshop. Then the agent handed me a form in which were stated the time I had worked and the amount I was to be paid. I was touched.

For my next task I had to go to a welcome centre at Schalkhaar. I had to interpret for a woman of the Galla clan who had lived near Afgoye. The fighters from the Hawiye clan had captured her and had locked her up with other Galla women in a military camp. They kept them there to rape them whenever they wanted, though they also forced them to cook, wash, and gather firewood for the soldiers. When telling her story the woman began to shake. She spoke in a very low voice, in short sentences, and when I tried to translate them I couldn't keep back my tears.

The story of that girl was indeed terrible. She had become pregnant in the camp and had given birth to a child. She always carried her child with her. One night one of the Hawiye soldiers snatched the child from her arms and threw it into the fire. He forced her to look while the child burned to death.

She was very thin. She said she was twenty-eight or twenty-nine, but she looked more than fifty. She spoke about all the other Galla women in captivity. She managed to escape when a different Hawiye sub-clan took charge of the camp; she didn't know what had happened to the others.

I told the Dutch female officer who conducted the interview: 'Please, forgive me. I know I'm not doing this well. I've begun this work recently and this is tearing my heart. I need a minute to go and wash my face.' But when she looked up I saw she too was crying.

Two months later I went back to Schalkhaar for another interview. The same officer, as soon as she saw me, came up to me and told me that the Galla woman had obtained the refugee status. We both smiled and congratulated each other. But by then I knew how many others had not obtained it." (Ayaan Hirsi Ali, Infidel, p. 326)

The writer went on to obtain a university degree, a seat in Parliament, and even, in spite of herself, to provoke a fall of the Government when her Dutch citizenship was called into question. The following remark of hers is relevant as her quotation of the government official embodies the point of view we are going to adopt in this book about second-generation immigrants:

"Job Cohen had been Vice-Minister of Migration Policy in Holland, and said that the problem was not so much immigration, as the astonishing inability to integrate the children and grandchildren of immigrants into Dutch society." (Ib. p. 387)

Many tears have been shed on the road to Paradise

and, at a more tragic level, many lives have been lost on seas and deserts on the way to a dream that never came true. The memory of so many victims of social disparity, daily renewed for us on this part of the world by accounts of such tragedies in the Mediterranean papers with their records of failed attempts to cross from North Africa to South Europe a sea that once was cradle of cultures and has now become watery tomb to many, lends a touch of seriousness and depth to the consideration of the oldest of human adventures. The human race progressed through migration, but it paid a heavy price for it.

THE VALUE OF PI

There is also a light aspect to the first immigrants' original plights to restore our views to balance and to hope. The following letter, a model in fiction of many such letters in reality, will bring a knowing smile to any settled immigrant's lips:

"Beloved Younger Brother,

Greetings to Worshipful Parents. I am hoping all is well with health and wealth. I am fine at my end. Hoping your end is fine too. With God's grace and Parents' Blessings I am arriving safely in America and finding good apartment near University. Kindly assure Mother that I am strictly consuming vegetarian food only in restaurants though I am not knowing if cooks are Brahmins. I am also constantly remembering Dr Verma's advice and strictly avoiding American women and other unhealthy habits. I hope Parents' Prayers are residing with me." (Anurag Mathur, The Inscrutable Americans, p. 9)

Another specimen among the abundant literature on the subject:

"When she got her daughter's first letter from America, the mother had a good cry. Everything was fine, the daughter said. The plane journey was fine, her professor who met her at the airport was nice, her university was very nice, the house she shared with two American girls (nice girls) was fine, her classes were OK and the teaching was surprisingly fine. She ended the letter saying she was fine and hoping her mother and father were fine too.

The mother let out a moan she could barely control and wept in an agony of longing and pain and frustration. Who would have dreamt that her daughter was doing a Ph.D. in Comparative Literature, she thought, wiping her eyes with the end of her sari, when all the words at her command were 'fine', 'nice', and 'OK'? Who would have imagined that she was a gold medallist from Delhi University? Who would know from the blandness of her letter, its vapidity, the monotony of its tone and the indifference of its adjectives that it came from a girl so intense and articulate?

The mother wrote back: 'Write a longer letter to me next time, my Rani. Try and write as though you were talking to me. Describe the trees, the buildings, the people. Try not to be your usual perfunctory self. Let your mother experience America through your eyes. Two years or even more for you to come back. How we worry, how we worry. You can't live on bread and cheese forever, but knowing you, you will. But you will lose your complexion, your health, your hair. Bathe every day. And don't get into the dirty habit of using toilet paper, all right?'" (Anjana Appachana, Her Mother, p. 1)

Once a bright student in my mathematics class at College showed me a geometrical construction of the transcendental number pi (3.14159...) he had found out for himself. It is well-known that pi, the ratio of the circumference to the diameter of a circle, cannot be expressed as the root of an equation with rational or even irrational coefficients. That's why mathematicians in all ages have excogitated geometrical constructions that cleverly approximate the value of pi. The student's construction was a very ingenuous one, surely beyond the capacity of an ordinary student, but he swore it was original. I showed it to the editor of our mathematics magazine in Gujarati *Suganitam,* to which I was a regular contributor, Dr. P.C. Vaidya, and as he also liked it we decided to publish it in our next number under the student's name.

A few days later, while I was reading the last issue of *The Mathematical Gazette* (a mathematics monthly from England), I found there the construction in question. Even the figure and the letters on it were the same. It was obvious that our student had read the magazine before me (praiseworthy initiative, to be sure) and had copied everything from there. I confronted him with the evidence, but he denied it. He insisted that his construction was original and declared that he had never read the magazine. Still, the evidence was such that in our next issue of *Suganitam* we just mentioned the information obtained.

Years passed by, and this good young man emigrated to America to continue his studies there. A few days after his arrival in New York he wrote to me a letter just to confess that he had in fact copied his construction of pi from that issue of *The Mathematical Gazette* years before and had lied to us and he was now sorry for it and apologised to us and to the readers.

What goes on in the heart of the emigrant on arrival at a distant land? What emotional shake-up takes hold of them, what heart-searching burns their soul, what moral crisis leads them to clean up memories and smooth out wrinkles forgotten in the depths of their moral conscience? The need to face a new life with a secure background leads to writing a letter and owning up a forgotten wrong. One needs all help of God and all backing of a clear conscience to enter the unknown, unfriendly, threatening world so different and so far. And the letter is sent.

Yes, my dear boy, be sure that we understand and forgive and forget and bless you and want you to succeed from the start and find your way and steady your step and bring to fruition in that new land all the talent we know you have and all the capacity to make reality the best dreams you dreamed when you left us in hope. And never mind about geometrical constructions for pi.

WHO AM I?

Indian sages have been telling us through centuries of meditation and wisdom that the fundamental question in our human lives, from which all others depend, is "Who am I?" From Sankaracharya's pilgrimages throughout India to Shri Raman Maharshi's smile at the feet of the Sacred Mountain Arunachala, the question echoes through valleys and consciences in the search of our true identity in the universe. That harmless looking abstract question was destined to become, across centuries and continents, the most urgent, practical, decisive and far-reaching search, not only in the metaphysical depth of spiritual seekers in Brahma's cosmos ever, but in the psychological reality of bona fide immigrants in first-world lands today. Who am I?

> "There is a part of me that's American and a part that's Indian. I'm clear about that and comfortable with it, except that sometimes people want me to be just the one or the other, depending on who *they* are. Indians who came over from the motherland [first-generation immigrants] have an acronym for my generation [second-generation immigrants]: ABCDs. Stands for American-Born-Confused-*Deshis*. *Deshi* here means Indian. I could tell some stories about *them,* like how they can think fair skinned equates with beautiful yet still make a big deal about colour prejudice in

America. But if it makes them feel better to call me confused, that's fine. The harsh reality, for them and for us, is that the immigrant never truly arrives but is in a constant limbo between two worlds." (Sohrab Homi Francis, *Ticket to Minto*, p. 134)

The interesting point here is the emerging difference between first-generation and second-generation immigrants in the matter of their identity as they feel it and as they express it. "I am an immigrant born in my own country" says an America-born son of Indian parents. "Two things are clear to me", another fine young man in the same situation told me only the other day over a non-vegetarian meal in a Madrid Italian restaurant, the Tattaglia, "Two things are clear to me. I am not an American. And I am not an Indian." What are you, then? The "confused *deshi*" (confused countryman) is not the America-arrived of the first generation but the America-born of the second. First-generation Indian immigrants in America knew quite clearly who they were. To the question "Who are you?" they would unhesitatingly answer, "I'm an Indian". No question about that. It was evident and spontaneous. At the back of their minds was even the notion that when retiring they would go back to India for a blessed old age in their home country. They felt happy to be in America now, and were quick in assimilating all new things around, but they were clearly and definitively from India. "I come from India." This was their obvious feeling and their direct expression of it. They were not in any way confused. But second generation immigrants do not "come from India"; they have been born in America. Or in England. Or in Canada. They want to identify with their new country and be taken as normal citizens like everybody else. Though they still "hail" in some way from India. That breeds confusion and blurs the answer to the vital question. Who am I? The spiritual, metaphysical, psychological question remains hanging in the air, and as there is no clear answer to it, there is no clear consciousness either of one's own personality and character and behaviour and destiny. If I am not sure about who I am, I'm going to be a bit confused about what I do. Indian sages did not insist on the question for nothing.

The main character in Hanif Kureishi's semiautobiographical novel "The Buddha of Suburbia", introduces himself thus at the beginning of Chapter One:

> "My name is Karim Amir, and I am an Englishman born and bred, almost. I am often considered to be a funny kind of Englishman, a new breed as it were, having emerged from two old histories. But I don't care – Englishman I am (though not proud of it), from the South London suburbs and going somewhere. Perhaps it is the odd mixture of continents and blood, of here and there, of belonging and not, that makes me restless and easily bored."

The author, born in England to a Pakistani father and an English mother, seems to reflect here his own experience of twenty years before, when he visited Pakistan after the success of his first screenplay, "My Beautiful Laundrette", and introduced himself saying: "I am an Englishman." All his kinspeople laughed, as they knew his uncles and aunts and all the family, and told him: "If you are an Englishman, we are American." He concluded: "I am in between." On London walls he had read the graffiti "Pakis, go home!" In "The Rainbow Sign" he wrote: "From the start I tried to deny my Pakistani self... it was a curse and I wanted to be rid of it. I wanted to be like everyone else." This can be the feeling of a highly successful second-generation immigrant.

Jehangir, a middle-aged Parsi successful in America

in Meher Pestonji's story, decides to go back to India "since he'd always felt a second class citizen in the US". (Meher Pestonji, *Mixed Marriage and Other Parsi Stories,* p. 139)

Two second-generation young girls are sitting with their father – who, by the way, had been Number One in the School Leaving Certificate Examination in the whole state of Gujarat in India – in the living room of their house in New York, watching the final decisive moments of an international game of baseball. With the last home-run, the American team achieves a narrow and spectacular victory. At that moment two simultaneous voices are heard in the living room. The father comments quietly, "They won", while his two daughters rise their arms together in the air and shout joyfully, "We won!!!" Identification with the new country begins to appear at home, and we find conflicting expressions of a changing attitude. These young persons feel American, talk American, think American, and want to be just part of the crowd, to be accepted as everybody else, to be taken as pure and simple Americans. But they don't quite succeed in that. Their name and their family, their shade and their features, their feasts and their visits to India remind them and their friends of their origin. There is no question of rejecting in any way their country of origin, they are rightly proud of it and love it and stand for it in every way, but there is definitely question of longing to be fully and practically accepted, to be integrated, to be taken for granted, not to be labelled differently, to be "like everyone else" as Hanif Kureishi has said. And that is not easily granted them.

The problem is not only for the immigrant, but also for all those who have spent the early years of their lives in a different country. India's "jewel" and first Prime Minister Pandit Jawaharlal Nehru, who, while being radically

Indian had been educated in England, wrote to his close friend Dhan Gopal Mukerji, the first Indian to become an acclaimed writer and speaker in the United States at the beginning of last century, in a letter dated 19 June 1928:

> "Unfortunately, I am a mongrel breed, neither wholly Eastern nor wholly Western, with the result that I seldom feel at home with anybody. The modern western-educated intelligentsia in India usually bore me to extinction. The poor peasant and the worker are loveable enough, but what the devil is one to do with them? I can't talk to them for long. So now I hope you will appreciate why I welcome your letters and will write to you frequently." (Dhan Gopal Mukerji, *Caste and Outcast*, Standford University Press 2002, p. 31)

This is a very significant letter, not only for its author but for its content. Pandit Nehru, such a highly intelligent Indian educated in England and now living in India, writes to an Indian born in India and now residing in America for understanding, sympathy, and mutual help to grow into their parallel situation. Both profited by their being rooted in two lands, and both contributed to enlarging the conscious experience of sharing in two cultures to the benefit of both. Nehru had planned having his biography written by Mukerji. They understood each other, and Nehru even became godfather to Gopal, Mukerji's son from his American wife Ethel Ray Dugan.

This historical remembrance is not without its pathos. "Revolution in India and depression in America, both took their toll of his mind and body until a nervous breakdown followed", wrote Mukerji's son Gopal about the addressee of this letter. Mukerji took his own life in New York City when he was 47. While this sad end was largely due to his own fits of depression, his failure to become a Ramakrishna monk in search of God, and the decline of his creative power with the ensuing financial difficulties, the shadow remains that the stress of blending two identities into one added to the tensions that provoked such an end. He was very dark-skinned – and very handsome indeed – and this was 1936. His violent death may be the reason why his memory seems to have swiftly paled into oblivion, but he was very highly and widely esteemed both in America and in India in his day. A noble pioneer.

> "During his lifetime, thousands in America and England had heard his talks, and he had attained phenomenal popularity. In only a few years he had jumped into public favour, and he had won the hearts of America's children." (Gordon H. Chang in Introduction to Mukerji's *Autobiography*, p. 26.)

I cannot refrain from giving a taste of his rich though now little known personality with some quotations from the autobiography of this genial and lovable man. They are both amusing and enlightening.

> "Once at Benares I stopped to bathe in the Ganges and I saw an old priest who had taken his bath and was meditating. Two Americans, a man and a woman, came along rushing. The man pointed his camera at him, and said reassuringly, "Don't be scared; it won't bite!" Then snapping his picture, he hastily put a coin in the old man's hand and disappeared as suddenly as he had come. The priest, who had been meditating upon the Lord, looked at the coin, then looked at the disappearing couple. In silence he threw the coin into the water." (p. 134)

> "One day I was waiting on the platform in a railway station in India. After three hours the train was heard. It stopped at a distance and the engine-driver whistled for the signal to come into the station. The

man who gives the signals was eating his dinner and he grumbled:

- What does he want, the fool, screeching like that?
- He wants a signal to come to the platform - someone said.
- Then let him wait till I've finished my dinner - replied the man crossly." (118)

"The reverence I felt for America was so great that nothing short of falling on my knees on arrival and kissing its soil would have sufficed to express my feelings. But Americans are a strange people! No sooner did they see that I had such feelings for their country than they began to knock it out of me in a very unceremonious fashion. The first American I met on landing was a man very quaintly dressed (later on I learned he was wearing 'overalls'), who had been sent to me to take care of my trunk. I gave him my trunk, which he threw from the deck of the ship down to the wharf – a matter of some eight or ten feet. Not knowing enough colloquial English, I quoted to him the magnificent lines of Milton:

'Him the Almighty Power hurled headlong flaming from the ethereal sky.'

The expressman looked at me very quizzically and exclaimed: 'Cut it out! You're too fresh!' This was my initiation into America." (141)

"Since I had come to acquire knowledge in America, I did not tarry in the seaport town very long, but hastened to Berkeley, the site of the University of California. I had no money except fifteen dollars that a friend had lent me. I went to the university hungry for knowledge, not knowing that knowledge, like bread, had to be paid for. So they took several fees out of my fifteen dollars under different pretences, such as 'non-resident fee', 'gymnasium fee', and 'infirmary fee', and to my great consternation, that drew my last dollar out of my pocket.

I kept myself alive on bread and water. Then I landed a job as a dish-washer. I stood silently for a while in front of the pile of dirty dishes till my employer came along and sternly demanded, 'Why aren't the dishes done?'
I said, 'How do you wash them?'
'Don't you know?' she asked in astonishment.
I said, 'No.'
'But', she said, 'you took the job on the understanding that you would wash dishes.'
'I will wash dishes if you will show me how', I replied.
Then in great dudgeon she said, 'Will you please look for another place tomorrow?'
'What place'? I asked.
She answered, 'I mean you are fired.'
I asked again, 'What is "fired"?'
And I was told, 'In good English, you are discharged!'
'But', she added with a smile, 'you can stay here tonight.' (143)

"America is a seed continent. All the world and all the nations are planting their best and their worst seed in this continent of springs. Asia has planted her mysticism, Europe has sown her seeds of diverse intellectual culture, and Africa has offered her innocence. America believes in herself. America was discovered in the name of India. Columbus, whose first name, Christopher, means 'the Christ bearer', set out for the land of Buddha – for India. He found instead a new land where Christ and Buddha shall meet. The voyage of Columbus ended in a mistake. The next five hundred years will prove that his error was an accuracy of the gods." (223)

These are prophetic words, and we seem to be in the midst of that prophecy. The world will be a better world when Christ and Buddha meet. Meanwhile we live under the stress of accommodating our step from the land of our birth to the soil now under our feet.

A young woman born in Kenya to Indian parents and now residing in London, writes these telling verses under the title "N.R.I.", that is Non Resident Indians, as people of Indian origin residing abroad are officially called in India, but which she interprets as *Nowhere Really Integrated:*

'We were not black enough to be black –
So Africa rejected us.
We were not white enough to be white –
So Britain is reluctant to accept us.

We were Asians,
But we felt more like
Foreigners in our own home.

We are British Passport holders,
Visitors to our Motherland.
This is the crisis between integrity and identity.

We are not totally Indian
Nor thoroughly British.

We are at the crossroads
Waiting at the amber light.
We are confused by the ascending red
And defused by the descending green.'

(Bharati Pankaj, *Slivers*, Kronos Books, 1997, p. 37)

Confusion again. It is not only that society discriminates against them and keeps reminding them in subtle ways and with nagging hints that they are different, but the more delicate and more intimate point is that they themselves feel deep down in their own being that they *are* different, that, in spite of all their efforts and their good will, they think differently and feel differently from their classmates and companions, and know themselves to be in some way special and particular and different. The tension is there, acknowledged or not, and tension always indicates a problem.

In the best of cases, even after the first shock, the sustained effort, the success, the acceptance in work and in society, there is always the lurking uneasiness of knowing oneself different, inwardly isolated, secretly discriminated against. Sharan-Jeet Shan, an Indian Sikh woman settled in England, writes:

> "I had trained as a teacher in this country and could never see myself as anything other than an individual as good as anyone else. But for most of my colleagues, I was always an Indian and an immigrant first, a teacher and a human being second. Successful integration did not mean mutual understanding, but compromising with the English point of view. As long as my opinion on any subject was not a deviation from the known variations on the theme, I was acceptable. Otherwise, one would have to stand alone." (Sharan-Jeet Shan, *In My Own Name*, The Women's Press, London 1985)

I was once speaking with an Indian friend in his office in downtown London. We were talking in Gujarati. At some moment in our conversation, his elder son opened the door, came in, and stood for a moment listening to us. Then he turned to his father and burst out loudly: "Why are you talking to your visitor in Gujarati? He knows English!" With that he went out in a huff and banged the door after him.

I want to understand that young man. Why did he

resent his father talking in his mother tongue? Precisely because he did not want to be reminded that his father's mother tongue was not English. His dress, shoes, hair, accent were those of any young man on any London street. He was totally identified with that society, and had achieved that identification with effort and labour through the years. At the same time he knew that this identification was fragile, delicate, weak, threatened by any hint of his family origin, by any slip that would betray his recent history and his different background. Thus the sound of the Gujarati language (which he fully understood) in his ears was a threat to his present status. It could reveal the hidden side of his personality, and that had to be avoided at all costs. That was why he had reacted so violently and had banged the door after him.

His impatience is understandable, but it is counterproductive. Immigrant youth who try to blend too fast with their new surrounding culture are those who do worst psychologically and socially, while those who keep attached to their own original culture do better, and those who become bi-cultural do best. Impatience for melting into the crowd may reveal poor self-esteem, insecurity, weakness; on the other hand, a strong attachment to one's origins does strengthen the present stand of the person, but it also prevents contacts for acceptance and growth. Either of the two extremes can be harmful. It is the double effort of preserving one's roots while putting out new branches that makes for organic growth and definite integration.

A WORD TO AMERICA

The important point that is emerging here is that when we speak of adaptation, inculturation, integration, these words and the processes they entail do not refer to the immigrants only, but, with the same force and to the same extent, to the people among whom those immigrants have come to live. They too have to adapt, to be integrated, to learn. In the new multicultural frame in which we are destined to live, it is not only Indians, say, that have to learn how to live with Americans in America, but also Americans that have to learn how to live with Indians in America; not only Turks that have to learn how to live with Germans in Germany, or Peruvians how to live with Spaniards in Spain, but also Spaniards who have to learn how to live with Peruvians in Spain, and Germans with Turks in Germany. It is only with this explicit, mutual, balanced and parallel approach that we can speak of adaptation, inculturation, or integration, and ultimately of globalisation, and the only way to make it work.

> "What we shouldn't do is to say that the immigrants should be more like us. We should construct a new us." (Prof. Robert Putnam, Harvard University, Financial Times, 20.07.06)

This quotation, in its conciseness, sums up this whole book and shows the way to personal growth on one side and to the establishing world peace on the other. "We must construct a new us". An "us" that may encompass both us and them. All. This is the challenge. The presence of immigrants among us, instead of making us withdraw behind walls and entrench ourselves in our own traditional way of life, has to prompt us and encourage us to open up in many ways and in many directions towards other worlds and other ideas we begin to guess in the gesture, the colour, the accent, the mystery of the whole human race which has suddenly stood at our door and is knocking for entrance. This is a historic phenomenon. A unique juncture in the development of humanity. A shining opportunity. A new dawn in history.

We have come to use the word "globalisation" to refer to this situation. But the word itself does not mean anything. When we say "globalisation" we have coined a word, but we haven't solved a problem. In fact, globalisation now is often a reference to a threat rather than to an achievement. Globalisation will only work for our good if we understand it as the mutual effort of the two sides who come into contact in any human context to understand, appreciate, befriend, cherish one another on equal terms, and go on in gratitude and wonder to know one another, to learn from one another, to grow with one another into new people with a richer mind and a larger heart. Both of them. The newcomer and the resident, the host and the guest, the visitor and the native, the black and the white, the North and the South, the East and the West. Both have to change. Both have to open, both have to learn, both have to grow. This is the secret of integration. Integration is never a one-sided imposition but a two-sided fusion.

This has not been clearly understood nor universally accepted, and therein lies the growing tension and the global menace of racial, cultural, and religious friction. The lifelong citizens of a country – forgetting that they often were immigrants in the first place – expect the newcomers to adapt themselves fully to the habits and values of the country they have freely chosen, and put on them the onus of conforming to the established patterns there, while they are in possession of the land and are only condescending to be good enough to allow the immigrants to come and settle among them. This attitude is unfair and it is at the bottom of the universal misunderstanding that is making cohabitation difficult around the world today.

> "Faced with the problems of cultural and religious pluralism, it would seem that neither assimilation of the new-comers into the receiving society nor their segregation into ghettos are the answer towards the integration of immigrants in the social life of their new country.
>
> Integration has to be proposed, not as a giving-up of certain attitudes of mind and behaviour on the part of the new-comers only, but as a two-sided integration or a plural re-integration in which we all, old-timers and new-comers, make an effort to shape ourselves into a new pattern of life." (Julio L. Martínez, *Inmigración, convivencia y pluralismo religioso*, Sal Terrae, Noviembre 2006, p. 232)

Again the same point. The whole point of this book. Two-sided integration. Old-times and new-comers. A new pattern of life. The forming of "a new us" that will embrace both of us, the responsibility of those who come and of those who receive them. We all have reflected long in books and publications of all kinds, in talks and conversation, in letters and articles, in private and in public on the attitude of the guest that comes, we have instructed them, groomed them, warned them, trained them to learn, to accept, to conform, to adapt, and all that is fine. Now it is time to instruct the host too, to make them realise they have their duty also in this matter, and this duty is not that of any condescension or benefaction, but the equal duty of brotherhood and cooperation, of teaching and learning, of giving and receiving, of sharing and profiting. Both sides as equals. Both changing and both growing. No vertical relationship but horizontal. Not one on top and the other below, but both at the same level. We all together are searching for a new identity that will benefit all.

Here comes my word to America. America is in search of a new identity, and this is her chance to discover it for her own benefit and the benefit of the whole world. I came to know America through Indian eyes. Born in Spain, I knew about Christopher Columbus and the new lands he set foot on, and nothing very much after that. My father, with unusual foresight in the nineteen-twenties, sent my brother and me to a German Kindergarten to learn German, the leading European language at the time, and engaged a *mademoiselle* to teach us French at home. He added, unsuspectingly: "English is not important. If you want, you can always learn it later in life." I learned English in India at a time when America was beginning to replace England as a political and cultural referent, and I spontaneously began reacting to American things as my Indian friends did. The common image of America in India became my own. I came to read *Time* magazine every week, *The Reader's Digest* every month, plus the printed luxury of *National Geographic* at times, and took for my spiritual readings the writings of Thomas Merton. I thrilled at Kennedy's election and grieved at his death, I worried during the Cuban missile crisis and saluted the first man on the moon, I hummed the songs of *My Fair Lady* and *The Sound of Music,* I learned to measure India's economic situation by checking in the daily paper the changing value of the rupee against the dollar. The dollar was the measure of all things.

Then came September 11, and all that world collapsed together with the Twin Towers. The smoking ruins were not only the ruins of concrete and iron, but those of an ideology and an identity. Who are we? A nation that was the ruler of the world, the arbiter of all conflicts, the trend setter, the undisputed leader, the '1' in international phone codes or plate numbers, the dreamt land of opportunity for the brightest young people all over the world... had suddenly become vulnerable, wounded, routed. The American way of life, pride and boast of generations, had been questioned, found wanting, defeated. Where were we now? Who were we?

The perplexity of a whole nation overshadowed the landscape of America. Self-criticism has always been a distinctive trait of the American character, and faced with the sudden collapse of its own self-image it searched in anguish for an explanation, a solution, a new image to project, a new identity to discover. This is the historic moment we are living today. Its importance, not only for America but for the history of humankind, cannot be overestimated.

And it is here where this book is proposing to make its humble contribution. America is searching for a new identity, is leaving the narrow frontiers of an exclusive club, is opening up to the opportunity, the newness, the challenge of new frontiers or rather of the disappearance of all frontiers, of new deals or rather the replacing of biased deals by open and equal collaboration. The moment has arrived for the construction of a new us, as we have been quoting here, the discovery of a new identity, the building up of a new personality. And this is to be achieved by the contact, the closeness, the openness, the assimilation, the integration, the help and the example of all the people from different countries, cultures, and religions that are now living by our side and sharing on equal terms our surroundings. Immigrants among us can help us, in friendship, in appreciation, and in trust, to find the best in ourselves by enlarging our views, widening our minds, and warming our hearts.

The WASP concept has been superseded. Colour (white), race (Anglo-Saxon), religion (Protestant) have ceased to be the coordinates to define the position of a person in society – if they ever were. Their ceasing is welcome, and that ceasing causes now the urgency to find new coordinates. The point is that the new coordinates are now multiple, the "multiple identity" we are going to propose in these pages, the enriched personality with all the cultures of history, the ecumenical attitude towards all religions in the world. And our immigrant neighbours are our best helpers in our search.

Together with the shock of the crumbling of walls all around us come the emergent values of a latent and promising fresh image. I sense in my American friends a sudden waking up to a new vision, a commitment to fairness, a sense of responsibility to the world, a desire to see, a readiness to change, a rejection of violence, a levelling of status, an unspoken tendency to bring the ideal and the working of democracy from its narrow practice within the country's frontiers to its welcome extension between countries in the world. We are all equal and no one is on top. Hubris, a Greek word which incidentally sums up the causes of the fall of the Greek empire, is being pronounced with awareness of the harm it has done and with the ring of considering itself now as rejected and abandoned. This is the emerging new identity in the thrilling process of its being shaped in the hearts of Americans and being projected as their new image to the world. This is the process I want to highlight and to define with hope and love. This is my word to America.

VEILS, TURBANS, AND PRAYER FACING MECCA

Once the main point has been made, I can proceed to illustrate the widening of identity with some concrete cases. Here is a practical example of the two-sided integration, which from this new perspective can be dealt with in friendship and peace: the Muslim girl who wears her veil at school. She has caused quite a stir throughout Europe. Conflicts, accusations, threats, defences, manifestations, opposition, confusion, legislation. A perfect image of the situation we are describing here. From our perspective now we begin to see our way to a solution. The decision on the veil should never be unilateral. And that is just the point. The Muslim girl in Europe must be sensitive to the reactions brought about by her wearing her veil to school; but then her European classmates must be equally sensitive to what the veil means for her and for her people in their hearts. After all we have discussed here it is easy to see that for her there is question of her identity. As serious as that. Her veil defines her before the mirror and before the looks of all as a true Muslim, and that is supremely important to her as we have seen when dealing with multiple identity. Her religious identity has priority for her and for people in her surroundings, it is a protection in a different and hostile world, it is a constant reminder of what she is and wants to be and should be at each moment according to the tradition that takes shape and winds itself around her head and her mind in the sacred veil. She has to keep that identity, and at the same time she has to widen it under the influence of her new surroundings. For her companions at school and their families and media people and the whole country in which she now resides the veil is a symbol of inequality of the sexes, of male domination, of the submission of woman to man, since men wear no veil while they impose it on the women. And the Muslim girl has to weigh this too in her mind before adjusting the veil before the mirror on her way to school.

It is up to the girl to enlarge the concept of her own identity, to keep lovingly her religion without having to advertise it on the street, to know herself as many-sided in a many-sided world, and to freely choose at each moment that facet of her personality that may represent her best and may bring her closest to her actual surroundings in any given situation. And it is up to her veil-less schoolmates to enlarge also their own concept of themselves, to appreciate the variety of religions in the world and the opportunity to personally know Islam with a Muslim friend in all its religious depth and its cultural tradition. The presence of a Muslim student in a European school benefits both the school and the girl. All are gifted with the chance to enlarge their knowledge and refine their feelings. The point is that the decision on the veil, different in each case and even in each occasion, should not be unilateral but shared. Let both sides come to know each other, to appreciate each other, to open up, to decide together. And then let both remain flexible to keep changing as they go on. Maybe the ideal would be, not for all Muslim girl students to wear the veil all the time and every day, but for each one to wear it or not to wear it when she judges best, in freedom and responsibility before the two cultures to which she belongs. That would be the way for all of us to keep on learning. And growing.

People in India have something to contribute to this controversy of the veil, and it would be good for their voice to be heard before the veils get too entangled. Some problems, actually, are not new, and the experience acquired in previous cases can help to tackle new ones with confidence. Men belonging to the Sikh religion wear turbans. The do not cut their hair, God's gift to protect us from heat, from cold, from bumps, from harm, which grows by itself up to a proportionate length, different for each person, and stops there. This religious reverence and ecological mindfulness leads to the preservation of hair in its natural growth, so that it is never cut in any way, and it is kept neat and bound inside an elegant turban. In India, with its majority of Hindus and large minority of Muslims, Sikhs make up only 2% of the population. And now to our point. They have to distinguish themselves from both Hindus and Muslims, and here comes the turban. It passes from being a religious symbol and an ecological tool to being a mark of a different identity. True, some Hindus use turbans even today, chiefly in the villages, but the shape, the style, the colour identify the turbans of the Sikhs and give them their exclusive, separate, recognisable identity. The turban, like the veil, is both a religious symbol and an identification mark. It is not a fashion or a whim; it is a definition, a commitment, an identity. Loud and clear. Historical and legitimate. Though the limitations we have taken note of in the matter of the veil also hold for the turban. If identity is reduced to a piece of cloth, we narrow its meaning and shorten its reach. If identity is enlarged to all its many facets, the veil or the turban would still remain, but not as a fixed, rigid, immovable object, but as one out of the many elements that form one's personality, that will blend and combine with all the other elements, and will come to the surface or retire to the background according to time and circumstance.

The Sikh are valiant warriors, and in the days when India was a British colony the British were quite interested in having Sikh soldiers in their armed forces. The army has always insisted in all its members wearing a uniform (uniform means uniform, of course, the same for all) but the cap or beret of the British soldier would not fit inside a Sikh turban nor the turban into the cap. The order was issued to remove the turban. The Sikh refused. The British priced more their military prowess than their own sartorial inclinations, and allowed the turban. It had to be khaki, of course, but it came to stay. And pointed, ironed, smart turbans can be seen when British troops march today to unending battlefields.

In more recent years a Sikh man in London passed all tests to be a bus driver in the municipality transport service. He was accepted but asked to wear the standard cap in the bus instead of his turban. When he refused, he was rejected. Driving a bus does not require outstanding courage like fighting in the battlefront, and the British Empire could well do without him. But he took his case to the court, and he won it. Since then turbaned drivers can be seen in the London double-deckers. Again, it is not so that all Sikh men always wear their turban. Some do not. Individual freedom is important in all cases. A Sikh colleague of mine in the Gujarat University in Ahmedabad, Dr Darshansingh, always wore a turban, while another Sikh colleague in the Vadodara University, Dr Ajeetsing, never did. Both were excellent mathematicians. And excellent persons.

Religious gestures are important, and that is precisely why they must be flexible and adaptable so that they can be maintained with ease in the midst of changing circumstances. A modern example has been provided by the first Muslim astronaut in the International Space Station, Sheik Muszafar Shukor, in October 2007. He is a practising Muslim, and he outlined from the start the difficulties he would encounter in his space mission. A Muslim prays five times a day, sunrise to sunset, but the Space Station in orbit goes 16 times a day round the earth in 24 hours, thus giving 16 sunrises and 16 sunsets, so that the astronaut would have to pray 80 times in 24 hours. Prayer has to be said facing Mecca... from a Space Station which changes its position at each moment. Before prayer hands, arms, face, head, feet have to be washed, and water is strictly rationed in space. And then prostrations and genuflexions could become cumbersome in zero gravity. What was to be done?

Muslim religious authorities carefully studied the case and very intelligently adapted the tradition rules to the special – and spatial – occasion. The time of the five daily prayers would be computed according to the hour in the Kazastan cosmodrome from where the space ship had been launched; to face Mecca it would be enough to face the earth from the remote orbit; the ablutions could be made in gesture only without water, as indeed it is done in the desert if prayer time comes where there is no water; and the prayers could be said standing. NASA accepted the astronaut's prayers, and the astronaut prayed with the new rubrics. When the two parties collaborate, both stand to win.

The capacity to adapt is the condition for survival and progress. Flexibility is always a sign of vitality. Congratulations to all. Sheik Muszafar Shukor can feel proud of his mission, as a scientist and as a religious man. Space pioneer in liturgy. Until them only the astronaut Fank Borman had openly prayed in space. He read from the space ship Apollo 8 on Christmas Eve 1968 the first ten verses of the Book of Genesis in the Bible. "In the beginning God created the heavens and the earth...".

As chance would have it, the Space Station commander on the occasion of Muszafar Shukor's flight was a woman, Peggy Witson. The Muslim astronaut was under her orders. Flexibility there too. Any organism that wants to stay young must remain flexible. Rigidity comes with old age. In the soul as much as in the body.

The more gifted the person is and the more they rise in the social scale, the more exposed they feel themselves to be, and therefore the more threatened by any situation that may jeopardise their unstable equilibrium. This may help us to understand, to value, to accept, and to help those who are passing through that stage in their lives, and can highly benefit society wherever they are, or, on the contrary, can become a danger to it if they themselves do not understand their own position and turn aggressive at feeling insecure. This we have to learn to avoid.

A BAR OF CHOCOLATE

Statistics bulge. The front page of the tabloid *"Qué!"* in Madrid on 04.02.08 blazed with the headline in bold type: "Immigrants are already a majority in a village near Madrid." In Fresnedillas, a village 30 miles from Madrid, the latest census gave 48% immigrants, which, together with an estimated 10% illegal immigrants out of census, gave them a majority. In the village school immigrant students made up 60% of the student body, from Rumanians and Bulgarians to Peruvians and Nigerians, with a variety of languages that made it necessary for remedial classes in the Spanish language. All that in a population of 1.472. Numbers sounded the alarm. The front-page headline loomed like a threat. It was a loud cry: Be on the alert! they are more than us! they are already a majority! The word "already" signals a process in progress that has overtaken us, will soon get farther ahead of us, and eventually will relegate us to a corner. They are already a majority! Get ready for the worst! Such sensationalistic slogans create an attitude of caution, tension, opposition.

A popular objection to the coming of immigrants is that they take away our jobs from us. Though we all know that as for menial jobs we, residents, do not want them, we need other people to do them for us, and we should be thankful to them for taking them up for us; and as for higher jobs we are inwardly grateful for the foreign contribution to the advancement of the country. Another objection is that immigrants bring with them different customs and mentalities and do not mix with us, and this is precisely what we are dealing with here. But two other points have to be dealt with here. Beyond these two objections there are other two, more subtle and more veiled, which have also to be considered now. One is that many of the immigrants are illegal, and if we welcome them we seem to help them to break the law and we encourage other illegal immigrants to come when they see how well we are treating those of them who went before, so that we would be contributing to the creation of physical and moral spaces outside the law. The other objection is that the blame of the poverty of the immigrants in their countries of origin lies with those same countries, with their extreme corruption, faulty administration, ethnic conflicts; and so the real solution for their poverty does not lie in helping those few that come out but the many that remain in those countries, urging for the lessening of corruption and the stopping of wars which are the real causes of their misery.

Yes, they are illegal. Some of them have reached our country breaking frontiers. But they have reached. They have arrived. They are here. Now it is for us to deal with them as we meet them on our streets and in our houses without starting an investigation on whether they arrived here with papers or without them. I give an example which may clear the matter. If I'm walking on the street and I see a motorcyclist without a helmet accelerating wildly, overtaking all vehicles, zigzagging on the asphalt, jumping red lights, violating all traffic rules…, and suddenly I see him losing his balance and bumping head on against a lamppost, I don't tell myself, "he is to blame, he has broken all the rules, he had it coming to him, let him look after himself now". I don't say that. He is to blame for the accident, to be sure, and I have seen it; he has broken all laws, but now he is a human body at awry angles with the pavement stained with his blood. I run to his side, I call an ambulance on the emergency number in my mobile phone and the police after that, and as I am a priest I give him sacramental absolution for his sins *in articulo mortis* as he may be a Christian and the accident may be mortal. The example is clear. Whatever the past of the person who needs my help, my understanding, my cooperation, I'll give it to them without asking for their credentials. It may be a motorcyclist on the road or it may be an immigrant on the market. The immigrant is here, he is my brother, she is my sister, and I will be by their side whatever the way they have arrived here.

Again, it is the situation in their countries of origin that is responsible for their having to risk going to other countries any way they can. This is also true. But I am not in those countries, I can't straighten their governments, admonish their politicians, convert their businesspeople to get those countries running well and efficiently. I only have my neighbour next door to deal with, and I want to do it in the best possible way, whoever they are and whatever way they have come.

Besides that, we are not quite innocent in our own countries with respect to theirs. We run them through centuries as our colonies and exploited them for our benefit without a care for their own welfare. It is enough to look at the map of Africa to realise that the frontiers in the whole continent were drawn with a ruler by European powers without any reference to races, languages, traditions, history, without asking the natives about it and without giving a thought to the consequences in cultural life and in social relationships. This colonial geography hurt Africa and made it into a continent divided by absurd lines, with ethnic groups separated on one side and opposed on the other, under a mixture of identities and a confusion of origins which lead to armed conflicts and permanent tension. All this unrest was kept hidden under pressure during European domination, and all this exploded suddenly into ethnic conflicts when the colonies became independent and different peoples found themselves bound and divided by artificial boundaries from north to south and from east to west in uneasy neighbourhoods. Wars broke out. Colonial heritage.

We watch films and read articles about diamonds born in the rich African soil and shaped by skilful hands, which are used to finance ethnic conflicts, to buy weapons, to feed armies, to lengthen wars. Luxury for blood. But then, according to those same films and those same articles, the businesspeople who buy and sell those diamonds in Europe are white, not black. And all the controls thought up to guarantee that the diamond bought by the millionaire in the north proceeds from clean and legal extraction in the south are systematically evaded along the whole distribution line as readily as they are set up. We are not innocent.

Africa is a sanctuary of raw materials. The whole world lives on them. A rich continent in its rivers and its sunshine, its soil and subsoil, its mines and underground, its forests and its wild animals. But the commercial protectionism imposed by the West to safeguard its own products automatically lowers the competitive value of products from poorer lands, and the subsequent elaboration minimises the importance of raw materials, the distribution net artificially multiplies costs, and in the end those who should earn most end up by earning least. We are not innocent.

I read the story of an American correspondent who travelled through several African countries to study the gap between the value of original raw material in Africa and the price of the finished product in America. He found that a chocolate bar that sold for two dollars in New York had given only fifteen cents to the farmer who raised the cocoa beans in Cameron, Nigeria, or Ghana. Unfair balance. But there was more to it. While on his field work, the correspondent one day sat down somewhere to rest, opened his rucksack, took out a chocolate bar and began to eat it for a quick surge of energy between tasks. Some people gathered next to him, and it occurred to him to take out another bar, break it, and distribute it among the children that were watching him with shyness and curiosity. But then he was not ready for their reaction. They put the brown bits into their mouths with suspicion, they waited for a moment to see how it tasted, they opened wide their eyes, looked at one another in surprise, licked their lips, jumped for joy, and put out their open hands for more. Then the penny dropped. He realised that those children had never tasted chocolate in their lives. The taste of the sweet was unknown to them. They knew cocoa beans, but they did not know Lindt or Nestlé or Hershey or Godiva chocolates. The plant belonged to them, grew on their soil, covered their fields. But they had never tasted the finished product. They instantly loved chocolate. And the hardened correspondent felt his eyes going wet. He had not anticipated this result of his research. He gave all his remaining chocolate bars to the children.

We at times resent immigrants. But we cannot blame them for their poverty. We all have contributed to it. We all like chocolate.

The wars. That daily horror. Stubborn news of blaring human failure. Open wounds on humanity's side that never close. And behind them, too, there is poverty. A poverty for which we all, again, are responsible. It is first priority to do all we can to reduce, counteract, stop all violence on the planet. Those wars and clashes speak of criminal acts that sadden our heart, and of victims who merit our admiration and respect, and inspire us to keep thinking and feeling and trying to heal the wounds of human coexistence we hear about and we share in grief.

> "On April 29, 1994, twenty-two persons, most of them school girls, were murdered during a raid on a girls Catholic school in Muramba, province of Gisenyi, Ruanda, close to the boundary with the Congo Democratic Republic. During the genocidal war between Hutus and Tutsis, a group of armed men assaulted the school and ordered the girls to divide themselves into ethnic groups, Hutus on one side and Tutsis on the other. The girls refused to do that, protesting that they were all one community and they loved one another. The men opened fire without discrimination and without mercy, killing sixteen girls and wounding fourteen.
>
> In the region of Kigali, Ruanda, where people of both Hutu and Tutsi ethnic groups lived together, war broke out and left in its wake blood vengeances everywhere. Neighbour attacked neighbour. In that place a Hutu man killed his Tutsi neighbour. Sometime later, after the Ruanda Patriotic Front had won the war and had taken charge of government, the massacres were investigated. The widow of the murdered man was asked to identify her husband's murderer. She knew who it was, but refused to identify him, as she knew that the Hutu man would be summarily executed. She chose pardon." *(Érase una vez África,* Joseph G. Healey, Mensajero 2007, 127, 123)

There is nobility in all hearts, and we all want to recognise it and to help it win the real battles of life wherever they are fought. And there are weaknesses also in all places, but they will not keep us from helping all people to better themselves and us with them. We are all together in this.

"I'M NOT A RACIST, BUT..."

Apart from wars, corruption, and illegality, there is a vague, general, dark resentment which finds expression in the dichotomous phrase, "I am not a racist, but..." followed by a complaint against something some immigrant has done which has rubbed us the wrong way. We are not racists, to be sure, but some racism from our surroundings rubs off on us too. We feel pity when we see pictures of suffering immigrants newly arrived at our frontiers, women with child, and children underage who have braved controls and faced dangers in their desperate effort to find hope for their lives. Our heart goes out to them and we feel ready to welcome them, help them, befriend them. But then we hear and see that once they have been met, fed, cared for, and admitted into the country, they soon become demanding and exacting, claim services beyond reasonableness, complain of lack of attention, accuse of discrimination those who attend to them, however impartially and dedicatedly they may be doing it. This hurts.

A surgeon friend of mine told me how one day in her hospital in Madrid two patients had to be operated upon, one an (illegal) immigrant and the other a Spaniard. The immigrant had to undergo a longer operation followed by hospitalisation in the same hospital for a week. The Spaniard needed only a short surgical intervention after which he would walk back home. It was evening, and, given the circumstances of both, the doctors decided to take the Spaniard first, discharge him in time for him to go home, and then take on the immigrant who would need a longer operation, would remain in the hospital for the night and so could preferably be taken last. On hearing this, the immigrant began to complain bitterly and loudly before doctors, nurses, and patients, telling everybody on the premises: "They are taking the other man first because he is a Spaniard. They always despise and ill-treat us immigrants. This is not fair and I'll lodge an official complaint." Which he then proceeded to do. The doctors felt sad.

I was once waiting before a traffic light while cars and motorcycles sped by in front when a saw a motorcycle overtake a car on the wrong side, swerve dangerously, bump on the car slightly and scratch its side with its mudguard without losing balance. The motorcyclist realised what had happened, looked back for a moment without stopping, saw the scratch he had made on the car, saw that the car stopped and the driver came out to inspect the damage done to his car, then sped away and was lost to sight. The motorcyclist was black. The driver of the scratched car looked up, straightened up, saw the motorcycle disappear among the traffic and shouted after the motorcyclist the instinctive insult against his whole race. Others saw the whole incident and nobody said anything. But one could read on their faces the words, "I am not a racist, but...".

On another day in Madrid's Columbus Square two young women approached me and asked me for directions to an address. They stood on both sides of me, spread out in front of me between themselves a map of Madrid and pointed on it with their fingers the place they wanted to reach. Tourists, obviously. I must have an innocent look as many people approach me on the street to ask for directions.

I always try to help, and will even walk a while with the inquirer if I can to guide their steps. I've often had to ask my way in foreign countries, I know the need and the gratitude of the stranger to the land, and I willingly help the visitor, the tourist, the immigrant. On this occasion too I tried to understand where those two charming girls wanted to go to show them the way on their map. They spoke haltingly in a strange tongue, they pointed very vaguely on the map, one of them one way and another the other. They were coming closer and closer to me on either side. I noticed an almost unnoticeable rubbing. And then – again – the penny dropped. I suddenly pushed out and away with both my elbows simultaneously..., and my wallet, which one of the girls was in the process of skilfully extracting from my trouser pocket, fell to the ground. They were thieves. Young, charming, expert thieves. They were experienced, and as soon as they knew they had been discovered, they flew in opposite directions to avoid persecution. I recovered my wallet, replaced it in my pocket, and stood for a while reliving the episode. A few passers-by who had watched the whole scene stood looking at me. One of them said: "Be careful. They were Rumanian gypsies." I love gypsies and I love Rumanians. But those two charming girls were not helping the immigrant cause. "I'm not a racist, but...".

Here I would also like to tell all immigrants that they can help us and make it easier for us to accept them if they behave properly among us. Not that they have to be models of virtue, which we are not either, but that they can avoid acts and behaviour which rub us the wrong way and do harm to themselves and to their fellow countrypeople whom we want to accept and to help. When they shout aloud to each other in the open street they irritate us. These are not our manners. We do not yell when talking to one another in public. Any lack of manners on the part of an immigrant becomes an offence. Some of our own people do shout in public too, and scratch cars and drive madly and cause accidents and steal and cheat; but the same offence committed by an immigrant hurts more and chafes more. You're a guest here. Please, behave.

Once I boarded a train in Madrid on a short journey. The seats faced each other two by two. *Vis-à-vis* they call them in railway language. A young man came in and sat by my side while the two seats in front of us remained empty. The train started. Soon the young man took both his feet, dirty shoes and all, and placed them irresponsibly, irritatingly, intolerably, flatly on the upholstered seat in front of him. The printed warning in red against placing one's feet on the seat in front was clearly visible before us with its evident drawing and clearly stated prohibition. I fumed but kept quiet. Better not to invite trouble. Least of all with a young man on a train. I felt like pointing out to him the red label and the obvious picture and shouting to him: "Please, don't place your feet on my furniture!" But I held back. Let's have the trip in peace. The train started, and after a while I thought of something. I quietly, peacefully, daintily, mischievously put my two feet, also shoes and all, on the seat in front of me, my legs in their angle perfectly parallel to the young man's legs. I said nothing and kept looking steadily straight ahead. He saw my gesture. He understood. He just smiled without turning his head and I saw him out of the corner of my eye. I too smiled without turning my head. None of us said anything. Then simultaneously, rhythmically, leisurely, playfully, we both lifted our feet from the seats, kept them for a moment in the air, and brought them slowly down together. And we laughed. Quite a ballet. You guess the point. The young man was black, and I was white. He was an immigrant and I was a resident. At that moment we had become one.

RECIPE FOR MASSACRES

When the bombs exploded in The Tube in London on 7th July 2005, the first shock we experienced was the violence, the bodies, the blood and the deaths. Photos and videos of the massacre filled our eyes and we shuddered at the mangled bodies and the twisted limbs among pools of blood. The worst sight human eyes can see in senseless violence against fellow humans. But then the second shock, beyond the blood and the massacre, in pure intellectual concept and mental understanding, was even more brutal and fierce in its cool realisation and its shuddering impact. The bombs in London had been placed by people born in London. Nice people, neighbourhood people, educated people, friendly people. They were second-generation immigrants, and as such were already taken as accepted, integrated, belonging. They had their families, held their jobs, drank their beer or ate their fish-and-chips like any Londoner at the next street corner. But deep down in their subconscious lurked still the nagging feeling, the jarring realisation that the equation was not quite perfect, that the equilibrium was not achieved, that dealings with "natives" were quite civilised but not cordial, that the cultural, emotional, political, spiritual gap was there, and was deepening, widening and festering. The wound was growing. And one day, under circumstances and coincidences and confirmation and organisation, the wound bled open. The time bomb exploded in their souls, and then it was only a matter of time before the actual bombs would wreak havoc in The Tube. The two bombs, the mental one and the dynamite one, are intimately related. Security videos showed later the London terrorists carrying on their shoulders on their way to their targets the heavy rucksacks with their deadly loads. Those were the material bombs. But those same people had been carrying for days and years on their shoulders and in their hearts the psychological bombs that were inexorably ticking away in their minds the seconds to death and destruction for them and for many. Those images were not reflected on the screen of any camera. But just as the police minutely examined after the events the several videos where the terrorists appeared on their way to their deadly mission, in order the better to understand the bombings and avoid their repetition, we could and should carefully analyse also the mental burden of many in similar circumstances, the resulting picture of their mentality, their chequered experience and their hidden feelings, in order to uncover the crises and frustrations, the anger and resentment that generate a hostile attitude in an originally friendly person.

This is not saying, not in any way, please, that every second-generation immigrant is a budding terrorist. Not that. But this does mean that the hidden uneasiness and weakened identity of a second-generation immigrant may unknowingly become fertile soil for protest, reaction, opposition, malcontent, hostility, manipulation and eventual violence. A study of second-generation mentality can help understand international terrorism. And understanding is the first step towards remedying. Therein lies the importance of this apparently simple finding.

We've thus seen how a problem of identity, Who am I? has become a problem of international security. Never did the Indian sages of antiquity suspect that their metaphysical search could have such practical consequences. Neither are we going to solve the riddle by lifelong meditations sitting in lotus posture under a banyan tree. But we have to tackle the concrete issue of belonging to two countries, of double nationality, of fidelity to two lands, of the burden and the privilege of carrying two cultures in one life if we want to understand one another, to enrich one another, to grow together instead of fighting against each other.

The dilemma is not solved by suppressing any of its two ends. An Indian who had become a successful diamond dealer in Amsterdam said plainly: "Don't call me Dutch, please." This did not imply any disparaging attitude towards the land he had chosen to live in and in which he was leading a happy life with his trade, his friends, his family; it simply stated a fact not to be hidden or ignored. I'm not Dutch. But then someone in the group told him friendly: "But you are not an Indian pure and simple either." And there were knowing smiles and nodding heads all around. We've met with Hanif Kureishi's formula, "I'm in between". This is a dangerous expression. It means "I'm neither the one nor the other", and it dangerously parallels the saying "to fall between two stools". To proceed by negation does not help the assertion that life is meant to be. Nobody can exist by default. Nobody can define themselves by stating what they are not. The true direction is rather the opposite: not to negate any of the two ends but to assert both.

Amin Maalouf, winner of the Goncourt Price 1993, was born in Lebanon, is a Christian, has Arabic as his mother tongue, lives in Paris and writes in French. He is thus fully qualified to write about the immigrant's identity, and begins thus his book in which, according to Le Monde, he "quite simply sets out what is required of civilisation in the third millennium":

"How many times, since I left Lebanon in 1976 to live in France, have people asked me, with the best intentions in the world, whether I felt 'more French' or 'more Lebanese'? And I always give the same answer: 'Both!' I say that, not in the interests of fairness or balance, but because any other answer would be a lie. What makes me myself rather than anyone else is the very fact that I am poised between two countries, two or three languages and several cultural traditions. It is precisely this that defines my identity. Would I exist more authentically if I cut off a part of myself?

So am I half French and half Lebanese? Of course not. Identity can't be compartmentalised. You can't divide it up into halves or thirds or any other separate segments. I haven't got several identities: I've got just one, made up of many components in a mixture that is unique to me, just as other people's identity is unique to them as individuals." *(Identités meurtrières,* p. 1)

And then comes the revealing intimate touch that opens up a whole new understanding in depth of the immigrant's self-understanding and points the way to the root of the problem and the solution to it:

"Sometimes, after I've been giving a detailed account of exactly why I lay claim to all my affiliations, someone comes and pats me on the shoulder and says 'Of course, of course – but what do you really feel, deep down inside?'" (p. 2)

This personal insight reveals the crux of the matter. Society does not allow us to have a double personality, to belong to two cultures, to benefit from two traditions. Jealousy is active in the best of relationships, and frowns at our having more when others have less. If I have two cars, and you have only one, you'll be jealous of me; and if I have two allegiances, two cultures, two languages, two countries and you have only one, you'll feel even more jealous of me, even if you don't consciously realise it, in a more subtle and devastating way, and you'll deride me, belittle me, will pat my shoulder and tell me patronisingly, "What about deep down there?"

Society is cruel. It does not tolerate newness, plurality, diversity, enrichment. It imposes routine, one-sidedness, uniformity, poverty. You cannot be different. You cannot be multiple. You cannot be richer. And if you dare, you'll pay for it. The pity is that this narrow-minded society has succeeded in getting its intolerant message across, and the newcomer hastens to forget himself and make others forget where he or she came from – unsuccessfully. This causes the tension and creates the problem.

> "The question 'What do you really feel deep down inside?' presupposes that deep down inside everyone there is just one affiliation that really matters, a kind of 'fundamental truth' about each individual, an 'essence' determined once and for all at birth, never to change thereafter. As if the rest, all the rest – a person's whole journey through time as a free agent; the beliefs he acquires in the course of that journey; his own individual tastes, sensibilities and affinities; in short his life itself – counted for nothing. And when, as happens so often nowadays, our contemporaries are exhorted to 'assert their identity', they are meant to seek within themselves that same alleged fundamental allegiance, which is often religious, national, racial or ethnic, and having located it they are supposed to flaunt it proudly in the face of others. Anyone who claims a more complex identity is marginalised. At present neither the law nor people's attitudes allows us to accept a composite identity tranquilly." (p. 2)

And then comes the shocking but thoroughly realistic indictment – as sad events have proved – of the limiting situation this intolerant attitude has led us to:

> "I feel like shouting aloud that this is how murderers are made – it's a recipe for massacres!" (p. 5)

From an identity crisis to the bombs in the Underground. This is the fearful link of a seemingly harmless question.

An editorial of the international Catholic weekly of London, *The Tablet,* strikingly traces the terrorist attacks in Britain to the crisis of identity in the second-generation immigrant as we are doing here:

> "Young Muslims are urged to volunteer for terrorist training or into terrorist cells in Britain out of their duty to defend the Muslim world, the *umma* [Muslim community]. What leads them to seek their identity in this arcane international concept – in some ways akin to the idea of Christendom in the Middle Ages – is the weakening of family and cultural loyalties associated with being a second-generation immigrant. They no longer feel as Pakistani as their parents did; they do not yet feel British. So they look to the *umma* to give them a sense of belonging. With the *umma* goes the notion of a Caliphate, ordained by Allah, to rule the world according to *sharia* law. They see it is their duty to fight for it, and there are no concessions the West can make that would placate them. What fuels their anger against the West is simply the fact that it is not Islamic." *(The Tablet,* 7 July 2007, p. 2)

"Being a second-generation immigrant." That is the problem. Neither Pakistani nor British. Then the lost identity is sought in the clear, shared, traditional, worldwide fellowship of the *umma,* and the strengthened links of the community accelerate the thrust towards religious conquest. Every Muslim in the *umma* firmly believes these three things: (1) Only Islam is the true religion. (2) The West is hopelessly decadent in its consumerism, corruption, sex. (3) It is the duty of every Muslim to bring the Quran to all for their own salvation. We, Christians, understand. Our Crusades in Jerusalem, our conquest of America, our Spanish Inquisition worked on the same principles. Outside the Church there is no salvation; all the non-Christian peoples are barbarians, pagans, infidels; it is our duty to bring them to the Gospel for their own salvation. Christendom in the Middle Ages. The Caliphate. History repeats itself. With about ten centuries in between. We can, at least, understand and help understanding. Understanding the problem is the first step towards solving it.

IDENTITY AND VIOLENCE

If the title of Amin Maalouf's book was *Identités meurtrières* (Murderous Identities), the title of another book on the same topic by Economy Nobel Prize 1988 Amartya Sen is *"Identity and Violence"*. Violence, murder, terrorism appear in both books as linked to identity. Violence is growing among us in the shape of global terrorism, and its immediate cause is misunderstood identity. That is the radical importance of our theme. Religion, language, land, race, history claim uppermost position in the definition of identity, even monopolise it in some cases, and that lopsided, stunted, partial, exclusive concept defines a person unilaterally against another person whose equally unilateral definition does not coincide with the first. A mistaken identity kills. Some quotes from Sen's book:

> "Violence is fostered by a feeling of a unique, unavoidable – and often belligerent – identity which imposes on us an extreme conduct – even an undesirable conduct at times." (p. 11)

> "Most conflicts and atrocities come from the illusion of a unique identity which does not allow choice. The art of creating hatred leans on the invocation of a supposedly predominant identity that smothers any other allegiance and which, adopting a belligerent attitude can overrule any human compassion or any

natural goodness we may possess. The result can be a crude violence at local level or a global terrorism active in the whole world. (p. 15)

"An important source of conflict in the contemporary world is the assumption that people can only be pigeonholed by their religion or their culture." (p. 16)

A unique identity creates division, opposition, conflict. Even it is the most important aspect in my personality, it cannot suppress all the other facets in my character, which at a given moment can be more useful and even more important to me. If I introduce myself as a Christian and the other person as a Muslim, we may feel some tension even under welcoming smiles, whereas if I introduce myself (as I did in an international mathematics congress) as interested in "finite Abelian groups", while the other expresses equal interest in "asymmetrical vector spaces", the smiles are genuine and without any shadows even if he is a Muslim mathematician and I a Christian one. Religion is, of course, more important in life than mathematics, but in this case mathematics is more helpful than religion. The same is true of music, sport, travel, hobbies or gastronomy. Sen enumerates multiple identities and applies them to himself in real life:

"In our normal lives we consider ourselves members of a variety of groups; we belong to all of them without contradiction. Citizenship, residence, geographic origin, sex, class, politics, profession, job, alimentary habits, sports, music, social commitments, among other aspects of the person, make us belong to a variety of groups. Each one of these groups to which the person simultaneously belongs confers on them a particular identity. None of them can be consider the unique identity or the exclusive belonging of the person." (p. 27)

"I can at the same time be an Asian, an Indian citizen, a Bengali with Bangladeshi ancestors, a British or American resident, economist, distant philosopher, specialist in Sanskrit, strong believer in laicism and democracy, man, feminist, heterosexual, defender of gays and lesbians' rights, with a non religious way of life, of Hindu origin, not Brahmin, not a believer in afterlife. This is only a small sample of the several categories to which I can simultaneously belong." (p. 44)

A researcher in relations between religions, Daniel A Madigan SJ of the Gregorian University in Rome applies this approach to our relationship with Muslims:

"One of the characteristics of the current negative discourse is that it tends to use the singular 'Islam' rather than the plural 'Muslims' and thus tends to ignore the extraordinary variety of views and types of people represented in the Muslim community. The sceptics are right to think that it is difficult, if not impossible, to dialogue with Islam – not just about religion, but about anything at all. That is because Islam is to a large extent an abstraction. There are many Islams – many ways of being Muslim in this world. Indeed, there are many ways of living one's willing submission to God even within a particular Muslim-majority culture. This is stating no more than the obvious, yet it is a fact that seems to escape so many sceptical commentators.

Our nightmare of ceaseless conflict seems to presume that anyone who bears the title 'Muslim' belongs to a different, irreducibly other, civilisation. The actual experience gives the lie to such essentialising discourse, and leaves us unconvinced that many of the world's 1.2 billion Muslims actually belong to the Islamic civilisation of our fears. If the puritanical and fanatical Wahhabis of Saudi Arabia and the Afghanistan's warlords and Taliban belong to it, then how can an urbane and thoughtful British professor, or a skilful and compassionate Malaysian doctor be said to belong to the same 'civilisation'?

Human maturity consists in the ability to negotiate this multiple belonging without losing a coherent sense of self." (Daniel A Madigan, *Salaam,* October 2007, pp. 141, 149, 150)

The last sentence shows the way to growth and peace in ourselves and in the whole world. "Human maturity consists in the ability to negotiate this multiple belonging without losing a coherent sense of self." To find the way to honour our multiple allegiances without impairing our individuality. We begin by finding out those multiple allegiances, recognising them, accepting them, combining them; we then move on to the task of defining which one of those facets of our being we want to come to the fore at any particular juncture; and then we go on to the more difficult venture of getting all those around to grant us the freedom to make that choice when we come to it. This can be a particularly difficult point.

"Nevertheless, even when we clearly see how we want to present ourselves at any given moment, it is possible that we may find it difficult to persuade others to see us in that way. Our freedom to assert our personal identity may at times be very limited before the others, who may choose to ignore the way we see ourselves." (p. 29)

A multiple identity helps the development of the individual and his relationship with others, while a one-sided identity creates conflicts within the person and with society. It is easy to see how reasonable and helpful this multiple way to see ourselves can be and should be, but then it is also easy to see that the way we usually speak – which reflects and reinforces the way we usually think – follows in fact the opposite approach, and the language we daily use takes for granted and strengthens the rigid and exclusive classification of humankind into separate classes. When we speak of immigrants from the south or from the east, of Latin American or African immigrants, we are being unfair to reality. Labels do no justice to anyone. In Latin America each country is different from all the others, even if they may have a language in common. Nicaragua is not Guatemala, and Uruguay is not Paraguay, and Puerto Rico is not Santo Domingo though I mistook one for the other on my first trip to the region and I almost booked my ticket for Santo Domingo when I was going to Puerto Rico. It's all the Caribbean, anyway. In East Europe a Rumanian is different from a Hungarian, a Russian, or a Pole, and in the Far East an Indian is not a Pakistani, and a Chinese is not a Korean. The blanket term "countries below the Sahara" is geographically, ethnically, and culturally unfair. We don't even properly know the names of all the countries in Africa, their boundaries or their languages. But each one of those countries has its own history, its traditions, its languages, its music, its customs, its art, its religion. Africa is a large continent with infinite riches in thought and feeling, in rhythm and colour, in wisdom and lore. The word "black" does not cover everything. The ebony face hides an infinite variety of souls behind features which to us seem uniform. But behind that apparent uniformity lie inexhaustible riches of all kinds of experiences, feelings, thoughts, and practices which are waiting for a friendly encounter to show themselves and to change the world. The list is unending.

"Defining a person as a member of a civilisation (the 'Western World', the 'Islamic World', the 'Hindu World', the 'Buddhist World) is reducing the person to a single dimension and to prepare the clash." (p. 70)

"The chances for peace in our world can well be reduced to the acceptance of the plurality of our allegiances and the use of reason that shows us to be fellow inhabitants of a vast world instead of prisoners rigidly packed in small containers." (p. 17)

The same Sen tells an amusing anecdote that frames his sensible arguments in the charm of his winning personality:

"Some years ago, as I was coming back to England after a short journey (I was at the time Director of Trinity College at Cambridge), the migration officer in Heathrow airport, who checked my Indian passport with undue severity posed to me a rather complex philosophical question. After looking at my home address in the migration form I had just filled up (Director's Residence, Trinity College, Cambridge), he asked me whether the Director, whose hospitality I was evidently enjoying, was a close friend of mine. I took a few seconds to answer the question as I myself was the director and I was not clear whether I could say I was my own friend. After some reflexion, I arrived to the conclusion that the answer had to be affirmative, as in general a deal with myself in a rather friendly way. Since I hesitated in my answer, the migration officer wanted to know exactly why I had doubted, and whether there was any irregularity in my entry in Great Britain." (p. 9)

A clear case of multiple identity. His passport made him an Indian, while his address as Director of Trinity College in Cambridge sounded British. Multiple identity always causes problems – sometimes for a moment only.

MULTIPLE IDENTITY

Maalouf again:

"How many of my fellow men share with me all the different elements that have shaped my identity and determined the main outlines of my life? Very few. Perhaps none at all. And that is what I want to emphasise: through each one of my affiliations, taken separately, I possess a certain kinship with a large number of my fellow human beings; but because of all these allegiances, taken together, I possess my own identity, completely different from any other." (p. 19)

This is a very rich concept. The more things I am, the more unique I become. Labels oversimplify and smooth away the edges, smudge the colours, level out the relief of the real picture. For practical purposes I have to squeeze telegraphically in the squares of an application form my name and profession and country and religion to define myself before bureaucracy, but I am much more than any of those framed words might suggest. Even my "Age" on a form does not define me, however mathematical its record may be, as people with the same age often are quite different in their maturity or their lack of it, in their looks and in their minds, in their health and in their outlook on life. Age is no measure by itself. And no other single feature of mine is.

I am many things and many people welded into one, I am all that I have gone through in my whole life to this day, whether consciously or unconsciously, and will keep on adding new facets, colours, nuances, angles and curves to my character with every event, every acquaintance, every circumstance, every experience that comes to meet my day any day anywhere.

There is the joke of the man in Ireland who had to fill an application form for a job, and in one of the dotted lines across it he was required to specify his religion. When he came to it he thought for a moment and wrote, "Agnostic", went on filling in the remaining lines, signed the form and handed it to the official in charge. The official scanned it quickly and efficiently till he reached the "Agnostic" line. There he paused, mused for a while tapping the table with the butt of his pencil, looked up and asked the applicant: "Yes, yes; this is fine; you've fully right to write what you've written. You are an agnostic. All right. But now, please, tell me: are you a Catholic agnostic or a Protestant agnostic?" The joke has its point. It is certainly not the same to be an agnostic coming from a Catholic background, an agnostic coming from a Protestant background, or an agnostic coming from an agnostic background. Though all those shades of meaning and of feeling do not fit over the dotted line on the application form. A single word will have to do for paper work, but it must not be allowed to rule the conscience and shackle the person. It must not be allowed to blur a personality before society.

The actor Orson Welles, on an American tour, was giving solo performances in which he recited passages from Shakespeare for a full session. To one of those sessions, only five people came. The actor came on the stage, took a good look at them and said:

"Allow me to introduce myself. I am an actor, writer, cinema director, stage director, architect, painter, an excellent cook, an expert in the *corrida*, magician, *connoisseur*, *enfant terrible*, and an authority on art. How is it that there are so many of us and so few of you?"

Having said that, he bowed to the audience and withdrew. He had personalities to spare.

Rodrigo Manrique, the hero of Salvador de Madariaga's best novel with the telling title "War in My Blood", is the son of a Spanish grandee and a native woman from a priestly family in the Mexico of Hernán Cortes. He is baptised a Catholic and brought up as a Spanish nobleman, but his Mexican blood surges in him, and he secretly returns to his ancient Aztec cult and his priestly calling. His Spanish ancestry also included Arab and Jewish blood, and when his father apprises him of that fact, he bursts into bewildered anger:

"What am I then? Even an Arab? Even a Jew? So many people in my body? So many races in my blood? Aztecs, Spaniards, Goths, Jews and Arabs. And does your honour still expect me to be in my senses and to behave myself? Who is going to rule so many people as your honour has put inside me? Shall I worship God or Allah or Yahweh or Uitzilopochtli? I don't know. I am a crowd."

Saleem Sinai, autobiographical character in Salman Rushdie's "Midnight's Children", expresses the same predicament in a different mood and a different language:

"Who-what am I? My answer: I am the sum total of everything that went before me, of all I have been-seen-done, of everything done-to-me. I am everyone-everything whose being-in-the-world affected-was-affected by mine. I am anything that happens after I've gone which would not have happened if I had not come. Nor am I particularly exceptional in this matter; each 'I', every one of the now-ten-hundred-million-plus of us, contains a similar multitude. I repeat for the last time: to understand me you'll have to swallow a world."

I am a crowd. I am a world. We are all manifold. And the more our facets, the more our worth. That makes up the uniqueness of our character in the multiplicity of our being. And that breaks the threatening monopoly of a single definition with an exclusive epithet. Maalouf once more:

"Any person of goodwill trying to carry out his or her own 'examination of identity' will soon, like me, discover that their identity is a special case. Life is a creator of differences. No 'reproduction' is ever identical. Every individual without exception possesses a composite identity. He needs only ask himself a few questions to uncover forgotten divergences and unsuspected ramifications, and to see that he is complex, unique and irreplaceable.

That is precisely what characterises each individual identity: it is complex, unique and irreplaceable, not to be confused with any other. If I emphasise this point it's because of the attitude, still widespread but in my view highly pernicious, which maintains that all anyone needs do to proclaim his identity is simply say he's an Arab, or French, or Black, or a Serb, or a Muslim, or a Jew. Anyone who sets out, as I have done, a number of affiliations, is immediately accused of wanting to 'dissolve' his identity in a kind of undifferentiated and colourless soup. And yet what I'm trying to say is exactly the opposite: not that all human beings are the same, but that each one is different. No doubt a Serb is different from a Croat, but every Serb is also different from every other Serb, and every Croat is different from every other Croat. And if a Lebanese Christian is different from a Lebanese Muslim, I don't know any two Lebanese Christians who are identical, nor any two Muslims, any more than there are anywhere in the world two Frenchmen, two Africans, two Arabs or two Jews who are identical. People are not interchangeable.

Few would object to what I've been saying. Yet we all behave as if it were not true. Taking the line of least resistance, we lump the most different people together under the same heading. Taking the line of least resistance, we ascribe to them collective crimes, collective acts and opinions. 'The Serbs have massacred...', 'The English have devastated...', 'The Jews have confiscated...', 'The Blacks have torched...', 'The Arabs refuse...'. We blithely express sweeping judgements on whole peoples, calling them 'hardworking' and 'ingenious' or 'lazy', 'touchy', 'sly', 'proud', or 'obstinate'. And sometimes this ends in bloodshed.

I know it is not realistic to expect all our contemporaries to change overnight the way they express themselves. But I think it is important for each of us to become aware that our words are not innocent and without consequence: they may help to perpetuate prejudices which history has shown to be perverse and deadly."
(p. 20)

Perverse and deadly. We are here confirming the

insight on the importance of this psychological discovery. We are many people. If we accept, understand, treasure this multiple belonging at the root of our character, we are on our way to widen our outlook on life, enlarge our conscience, enrich our personality. It is the way of growth, of personal integration, of international peace. On the other hand, if any individual or any group reject this open approach to self-understanding and social relationships, if they disown even a dual belonging, a twin heritage, a simultaneous allegiance to two cultures, two traditions, two countries, and narrowly define themselves as exclusive members of only one group geographically or ideologically, they are grievously limiting their own personal development as human beings, and are potentially becoming a threat to friendly coexistence and world peace. "This is how murderers are made." "Perverse and deadly."

> "Each of us should be encouraged to accept his own diversity, to see his identity as the sum of all his various affiliations, instead of as only one of them raised to the status of the most important, made into an instrument of exclusion and sometimes into a weapon of war. Especially in the case of those whose culture of origin is not that of the society they live in, people must be able to accept a dual affiliation without too much struggle; which means remaining loyal to their culture of origin and not feeling obliged to conceal it like some shameful disease, and at the same time being receptive to the culture of their adoptive country." (Maalouf, p. 159)

A smile to lighten up the discussion. When Winston Churchill paid his first official visit as Prime Minister to the United States, a newspaper correspondent brought out the point that his maternal grandmother had been an American, and so Churchill himself was, the correspondent said, "25 per cent American". Churchill answered instantly with his ready wit and unfailing repartee: "Yes, sir. I'm 25 per cent American..., and 100 per cent British!" And never mind the algebra.

MONSOON WEDDING

The desire many immigrants experience to forget their country of origin and have it forgotten by their new acquaintances in a distant land may stem from a sense of inferiority coming from originally belonging to an "underdeveloped country" while now living in a "first-world country". Colonialism, economic differences, psychological complexes, and simply systematic propaganda on the part of the rich countries have succeeded in creating a false sense of superiority of the West over the East which extends itself from table manners to religious beliefs and from literature to industry, and makes the new arrivals from the Far East to feel uneasy and humbled before the glamour, the cleanliness, the efficiency, the self-confidence, the pride and the growth of the lands of the West. This superiority is deceiving, of course, but it has been taken for granted, accepted, inherited by both "superiors" and "inferiors", and explains why the immigrant has often wanted to have their past forgotten as soon as possible and their new cultural outlook to be projected all around themselves for their own safety and satisfaction. The tendency to reject one's past is regrettable but understandable.

Curiously and ironically, as far as financial welfare is concerned, several Eastern countries are now forging ahead of traditionally advanced countries in Europe, and so the tables are being turned, and the economic basis for self-respect and self-assurance is shifting fast from West to East and creating a new confidence and optimism in the emerging economies of the fast growing countries. However, this is not the point. Self-esteem and self-confidence must not be based on the exchange rate of the dollar or the euro with the *rupee* or the *yuan*. Even the poorest country has a rich culture, and even an illiterate person can be a carrier of an ancient heritage. And this is what counts. We all can give and we all can receive. Two-way traffic is the policy without bias and without prejudice. Reciprocity is the answer. The best way to grow ourselves and to help others grow to the advantage of all is telling simply and unobtrusively to people around, through contact and presence, in the office and on the playground, what we think and feel and are ourselves, and listening to all the others with open ears and open mind, without any inferiority or superiority complex, as we plainly and directly interact with others in word and in gesture. Nobody is better and nobody is worse, but we all have ideas, traditions, customs, beliefs that are meaningful and practical, and can help enlarge, complete, enrich the ideas, traditions and beliefs of other groups, as their attitudes can enrich ours. It is this balance in ideological exchange that is the basis for a significant and beneficent meeting of cultures.

Kishore Mahbubani, in a book with the threatening title "Can Asians Think?" senses that this balance of exchange is beginning to take place with a new "two-way flow" of ideas between East and West for the first time in history as I have just said it should be:

> "If my intuition is proven right, we will begin to see, for the first time in five hundred years, a two-way flow in the passage of ideas between the East and the West early this century. The world will be a much richer

place when Western minds stop assuming that Western civilisation represents the only universal civilisation. The only way that the Western mind can break out of its mental box is to first conceive of the possibility that the Western mind may also be limited in its own way." (p. 9)

To be limited means two things: one *has* something; and one does *not* have everything. And that is true of all of us. So we all can treasure what we have and be ready to share it with others, as we are at the same time reminded that we don't have everything and will do well to open up before others to receive inputs from them. To be only at the receiving end is a sign and a cause of inferiority, while healthy give-and-take is the way for mutual understanding and growth. I underline the sentence: "The world will be a much richer place when Western minds stop assuming that Western civilisation represents the only universal civilisation."

An outstanding example of integration in a new culture has been given to the world by Indian writers settled in English-language countries and writing in English for a world reading public. They preferably choose for their tales Indian themes, characters, names, which they know best and can present with advantage to a general public, but then they write in idiomatic, local, colourful, masterful English. This is no mean feat. They are not afraid to present to Western readers the inside of an Indian family, and they do so with a mastery of English which brings to the literary scene familiarity of style together with the novelty of argument and situations. No wonder they have won prizes and multiplied editions, and are enlightening and entertaining readers the world over. It is a pleasure to any knowledgeable reader to follow the intricacies of the Ganguli family "from their tradition-bound life in Kolkata through their fraught transformation into Americans" as the jacket blurb of Jhumpa Lahiri's novel "The Namesake" proclaims, while we learn or are reminded along the text of the etymology of each Indian name, since Ashoke means "without grief", Ashima means "without limit", and Moushumi means "monsoon breeze". Sheer cultural delight. This is a pattern of what could be done in other fields bringing Indian seeds to fertilise faraway lands. It has also been successfully done in the field of the filming industry. Lila Nair's film "A Monsoon Wedding" is a treat I've seen enjoyed by people of quite different lands and quite different cultures. "Rain is coming..., and so is the Family." Just laugh and relax. Even if you know nothing about the meaning of *muhurat* or *hastamelap*.

Yashmin Hai is the daughter of Muslim Pakistani parents with Urdu as her mother tongue, but born and educated in London. Her father insisted that all his children had to learn English, learn and adopt English ways and manners, should become fully and definitely British. She charmingly tells her own transformation since her childhood:

> "I soon cottoned on to the idea that there was something now that one had to 'become'. We were not there yet. But it was understood that, by working hard, we could get there. I later learnt a word for 'this' thing that you had to become, 'this' place you had to get to. It was called 'English'.
>
> 'Ahh!' my father and his friends would say admiringly to each other whenever English manners, English clothes, English education, English toys, etc., were mentioned. English, it seemed, was something good, something to be proud of. In fact 'English' sounded so nice that when I imagined what it could look like,

I would see a bright, white light and I would hear the comforting sounds of children laughing and playing. I once told my mother my description of 'English'. She looked at me slightly bemused, before returning her attention to Farah, my newly born baby sister.

The discovery that the neighbours on both sides of our house were white delighted me. Perhaps, if I observed them carefully, I might learn what 'being English' exactly meant." (The Making of Mr Hai's Daughter, Becoming British, Virago Press, London 2008, p.37)

One guesses the first problem. Her mother. Her original language was Urdu, and she had learned some English but not much. Her husband, once in London, decreed accordingly that she should speak Urdu at home so that their daughters would not entirely forget their mother tongue, and they would speak to her in English to improve the knowledge of the new language for her. Very clever, but it didn't work. Or rather, it worked but with a great loss on the other side.

"Over the next few months we did gradually stop speaking Urdu. It wasn't hard – I didn't even miss it. If we ever did slip up, my father was always on hand. 'Ahh, uh, not in Urdu, in English please', he would say. We would quickly correct ourselves.

My father was right – our English did improve. My mother's English got better too. She was very pleased with her progress. And so were we. But something else changed once we dropped Urdu, something quite fundamental. It just became too frustrating trying to explain complex matters of the head and heart to my mother in English. After dropping Urdu, she became lost to me for ever." (60)

To the language were gradually added British customs, manners, attitudes, opinions that identified them more and more with the English middle class among which they lived.

> "The funny thing about our discussions [on any point] was that they were also helping us realise just how British we actually were. They revealed to us that we were forging our own history in this country. That somehow, we belonged here. Britain was our only home." (216)

Years pass, she grows up though she has not got married, her father expires. Her relationship with her mother becomes strained. Temper, tension, quarrels. They discuss her future on the phone, and her mother tells her:

'You know what your problem is?'

'What?'

'Your father gave you too much freedom. Now you've seen too much.'

'What does that mean?' I said, my voice starting to shake at the mention of my father. In one quick swipe my mother had taken our argument to a darker level. She had reminded me that the freedoms my father had given me were taking me farther away from my roots and, more importantly, from her. In the past, I had avoided thinking about these issues, choosing to believe that I had successfully found a balance between my two lives. But now – with questions over my future reaching some sort of climax point and with some difficult decisions needing to be made – I no longer could.

'Hello, are you there?' I heard my mother whisper.

'Got to go', I cried, quickly putting the phone down

before my emotions got the better of me. It was only when I put the receiver down that I realised my mother had been choked up with tears, too.

That evening, for the first time ever, I found myself questioning my father's ideas and how he had chosen to bring us up. All my life I had blindly followed him. When he had ordered us – as children – to be English, we had become English. When he had demanded we drop our mother tongue, we had dropped our mother tongue. When he had encouraged us to go out into the open world and be independent individuals – well, that is exactly what we had done. But what peace had his ideas ever brought me? None at all.

Hard as it had always been to admit, I knew I was never going to lead a life that my mother could be totally part of. We were too different. I would always be an outsider in my mother's world and she an outsider in mine. My mother was right, I had seen too much. There was no going back for me. And, whether I liked it or not, she would end up living on her own: being distant from me.

I wanted to be angry at my father for the situation he had put us in, but I knew it was pointless. He was dead." (266)

Poignant description of what many feel and few express. The uneasy standing of the second-generation immigrant between two cultures and two allegiances. Yashmin's parents did not have that problem in their past, and her children will not have it either in their future. Her parents, in spite of her father wearing a tie and her mother giving up the veil (which created quite a scene in their London home when she refused to remove it and her husband threw all her veils into the fire) were still

Pakistanis at heart while her children will just be British. But she belongs to the second generation, to the in-between generation, astride between two cultures, two languages, two religions, feeling all the strain and bearing all the brunt. They deserve our full understanding and caring.

WHY INDIA SPLIT

The immigrant's greatest privilege is to possess two languages. Though often the very immigrant is not aware of that blessing and does not appreciate it or benefit from it as they should. Two languages means two minds, two cultures, two souls. This is an intellectual luxury and a cultural boon which, if properly understood and put to use, can enrich one's life beyond the wildest dreams. One language learned from birth with all the implications, memories, emotional resonances and historical legacy of a mother tongue, and another language now used daily among people for whom it is the expression of their character, their instrument of work, their national identity and their link to the world. If this does not enlarge the mind, multiply viewpoints, open up horizons and heighten sensibility, nothing else will.

Here, again, first-generation immigrants laboured under the complex of not quite mastering the idiom and the pronunciation of English on arrival at "foreign" as they would say, and experiencing language as a barrier and an obstacle rather than a bridge and a link; while the second-generation immigrant has fully mastered the new language having learned it from birth, and speaks it now "like one to the manner born". They can even feel embarrassed when they hear their parents pronounce English before others with a heavy Indian accent which they have come to recognize as bizarre and to eschew as a speech blemish and an awkward reminder of their different origin. When Karim Amir in Hanif Kureishi's autobiographical novel, is offered his first job which consists in acting Mowgly in a stage version of Kipling's "The Jungle Book", and, to make his character true to life is asked to speak English with an Indian accent, he explodes, "I can't do this!", as it would be a reverting to his previous identity, a loss of the personality he had painstakingly acquired, a step back. You cannot ask an Indian who has mastered the Queen's English to mimic the accent of a local Indian even in jest. Don't rub it in.

I treasure the anecdote of Mumbai born Hawthornden Prize winner late Dom Moraes who was loitering alone one night through London streets when a "bobby" approached him and noticing his colour asked him routinely, "May I see your papers, please?" Dom Moraes drew up to full height, squared his shoulders, looked the policeman in the face, put on his best cockney accent and exclaimed with feigned surprise, "Oh, no, real-ly?" Upon which the policeman smartly saluted him and excused himself. "Sorry, sir". The proper accent is more effective than a passport. In fact it *is* a passport to instant recognition and social acceptance.

Karim Amir's father had actually forbidden him to learn Urdu. That shows the eagerness of a father to get his son integrated and accepted in the linguistic community without any hitch. This is an understandable attitude as well as a thoroughly mistaken one. A language is a treasure. Anybody in the West would give anything, and indeed many take great trouble and put in serious efforts, to learn and master an "exotic" language, and would benefit by it in their personal development and boast of it in their social circles as it would be a prized asset in anybody's cultural curriculum. A second-generation Indian immigrant, while been quickly immersed in the language of his adopted country from classroom to hit songs, still hears their parents' language at home, knows the alphabet, reads the script, and can even follow the dialogues of Hindi movies on DVD.

Once in London I was scheduled to have an interview by BBC radio on the phone in the Gujarati language, and I was told to be ready exactly at 6:10 p.m. when the phone call would come. It came. I took it. I answered directly in Gujarati to greet the caller and tell him I was ready to begin the interview when he would tell me. There was a pause at the other end. Then a voice, in the deep and rich BBC accent and the varied, wavy intonation we from oversees identify with awe and reverence with the best Queen's English, said: "I'm so very sorry I'm not conversant with your language, sir. I would love to speak it indeed! Please accept my apologies, and now I'll pass you on to the Indian broadcaster who is eager to conduct your interview." In the interview I took the opportunity to tell this very story and then to add: "Here is an Englishman who would give anything to know our language, and you have it in your hands and are throwing it away thoughtlessly!" I hope listeners got the point.

In families hailing from India and settled abroad we have today a generation of young people who understand their parents' Indian language easily, speak it hesitantly, read it reluctantly, and write it incorrectly. The linguistic downward trend in home languages has thus been initiated and will inexorably lead to the disappearance of all those languages from Indian homes in Europe or America in a very short generational period. This will be nothing short of a tragedy. An Indian language comes easily to an Indian emigrant, and it would be a tragedy if they would let go of the treasure that is still theirs and that others would love to possess. We have seen and we understand the need and the hurry for linguistic acceptance the immigrant feels, and we approve of their zest and effort in grammar and accent, but we regret the misguided zeal with which at times they prize so highly their new language that they look down on their old one. The need to identify with an English speaking crowd, the eagerness to show how well one knows English, even the lurking shame of falling back on "third-world dialects" can hold tongues and erase memories with frightening ease. The coming years may see the disappearance of Indian languages from homes where they were still spoken till recently, and that would be a great loss, not only for India but also for the world. The world needs increasingly people who may be at home in two cultures, and that implies two languages, in order to effect the rapprochement and the unity between peoples humankind badly needs at this juncture in its history, and it would be a great pity if those who already posses that precious qualification would lose it.

What is needed to keep home languages alive is not precisely institutions or textbooks or courses or examinations, but simply a change of attitude towards them. Instead of undervaluing, suspecting, rejecting them, we should value them, prize them, treasure them, and just gently profit by the occasions offered by family life, contact with elders, visits to India, books and magazines in Indian languages and religious functions requiring sacred expressions untranslatable into English. Languages enter by the ear, and in transitional generations of immigrants there are still sufficient auditory inputs to provide a basis on which a practical knowledge of the language can be built.

Language can change a life. It can even change history. Muhammad Ali Jinnah, Pakistan's Quaid-e-Azam, Father of the Nation and architect of Pakistan's independence, came from a Gujarati Ismaili Khoja family, and so when Gandhiji, who was also a Gujarati, met him for the first time in India on his trail towards Indian independence when India was still one from Rawalpindi to Kanyakumari and from Dacca to Karachi, he spoke to him in their familiar informal Gujarati. Jinnah answered him in stilted English.

- *Kem ccho, bhai, majaman?* [How are you, brother; fine?]
- I beg your pardon?

The curt dialogue had settled the fate of the subcontinent. When, soon after that, Gandhiji was given his first public reception by the Gujaratis of Mumbai, the split became public. This is how Gandhiji himself tells it:

> "The receptions in Bombay gave me an occasion for offering what might be called a little Satyagraha [peaceful opposition]. At the party given in my honour at Mr Jehangir Petit's place, I did not dare to speak in Gujarati. In those palatial surroundings of dazzling splendour I, who had lived my best life among indentured labourers in South Africa, felt myself a complete rustic. With my Kathiawadi cloak, turban and dhoti, I looked somewhat more civilized that I do today when I go about half naked, but the pomp and splendour of Mr Petit's mansion made me feel absolutely out of my element. However, I acquitted myself tolerably well, having taken shelter under Sir Pherozeshah's protecting wing.
>
> Then there was the Gujarati function. The Gujaratis would not let me go without a reception, which was organized by the late Uttamlal Trivedi. I had acquainted myself with the programme beforehand. Mr Jinnah was present, being a Gujarati, I forget whether as president or as the principal speaker. He made a short and sweet little speech in English.

When my turn came, I expressed my thanks in Gujarati explaining my partiality for Gujarati and Hindustani, and entering my humble protest against the use of English in a Gujarati gathering. This I did, not without some hesitation, for I was afraid lest it should be considered discourteous for an inexperienced man, returned home after a long exile, to enter his protest against established practices. But no one seemed to misunderstand my insistence on replying in Gujarati." (The Story of My Experiments With Truth, Beacon Press, Boston, 1995, p. 374)

At least one person had certainly misunderstood Gandhiji's gesture. Or, more truly and significantly, had perfectly understood it with all its consequences, and Partition had become unavoidable. Two languages meant two nations. Two languages, in mind and in dictionary. And, hence, in history and geography. Who knows, if Jinnah, in their first meeting, would have answered Gandhiji in Gujarati, maybe India would not have split. After all, the two leaders were Gujaratis. I beg your pardon?

STATION COMING

One day after my first arrival in India I wanted to find my way to the railway station in Mumbai, and I asked in English a passer-by for directions. He helpfully and repeatedly pointed with descriptive gestures the different turns I had to take while he enlightened me in English: "Straight, straight. Traffic island coming. Turn left. Big fountain coming. Then straight, straight. Station coming." I followed his instructions and I successfully reached the railway station. Together with that I also got my first field lesson in applied linguistics. My informant was speaking to me in English, but was mentally translating from his own Indian mother tongue and keeping its idiom. Now, as I was to discover later, in Indian languages things and places "come to us" instead of our "going to them". When our train is approaching Mumbai, we say in English: "We are reaching Mumbai." In Gujarati we say: "Mumbai is coming."

This is not only an expression of the relativity of all movement, but a fundamental difference in outlook and philosophy which lies at the basis of all Indian thinking, and is rich in consequences and applications. And that difference is clearly reflected in the language. I was walking to the railway station. But it was the railway station that was coming to me. What was the lesson behind the idiom?

School children in India innocently translate the English expression "We walked till we reached the river" too literally as "Walking walking river came". We are doing the walking but it is the river that is coming to us – water and all. We are not going, doing, achieving things, but things and situations and objectives come to us, meet us, happen to us. A whole family is planning to go to the movies on Sunday evening but they are not sure whether they'll get tickets for the show. They send their best boy to the cinema, he stands in the queue, waits impatiently, holds the money, finally gets the tickets, runs home and announces the good news to all. What expression does he use? In English he would shout triumphantly while he waived the prized tickets in his hand: "I got the tickets!" In Gujarati he just announces with cool detachment: "The tickets have come." After all the heat, the time, the money, the effort and the energy used up in getting the tickets in hard competition for a popular movie on a Sunday evening, his final statement to sum up the whole experience is: "The tickets have come." The tickets – like the railway station – come to us. They come to us, as it were, almost by themselves. They come to us because they had to come, because it was so determined, because it is not our money or our effort or our perseverance that matter, but the fact that the order of this world and the running of daily events is ruled by our destiny, our past actions, our merits and demerits, the divine order of providence that is responsible for the events in our lives and in the universe, our karma. The tickets *had* to come, whether we knew it or not. Now they have arrived, and that is all there is to it. "The tickets have come." Let's go and enjoy the movie.

There's more to come. In Western thought the subject bears the responsibility for their actions, and this moral responsibility is translated into the grammatical responsibility of the nominative which heads and governs the sentence. Thus, in English, "I do, I act, I get, I achieve...", and whenever the first person singular is acting, the "I" will dominate the scene and rule grammatically the verb – including the oddity of its being spelt with a capital "I" – and has the verb agree with it in number and person. Here Indian languages are keeping a good surprise for us. The English "I know" becomes in Gujarati "to me there is knowledge"; "I enjoyed myself" is "enjoyment fell upon me"; and "I got a job" means only that "a job met me". "I am afraid" is "to me there is fear"; "I liked it" is "it is liked unto me" or "to me there is liking"; "I got angry" is "anger came to me", or "climbed upon me". The list is endless. Behind all these examples and innumerably many others is the fact that can be simply and tellingly stated thus: where English uses the nominative "I do", Gujarati uses the dative "it happens to me". Quite a linguistic upset.

If I forget something, I need not say with a touch of repentance and embarrassment, "Oh, I'm sorry, I forgot!" but I have only to state the fact that "Remembrance did not come to me". If the memory did not come, it is its fault, not mine. Nothing for me to feel sorry about. And the same situation obtains if I don't like something I should like or I feel jealous when jealousy only "climbed on me". There is no question of passivity or lack of responsibility here but of mental equilibrium and spiritual detachment. We in India are keenly aware of whatever is happening to us, know ourselves to be in the midst of a current of life that advances by itself unremittingly all around us, realise that most events are not in our hand, as indeed they are not, and so we allow to happen to us, always under our own direction, acceptance and choice, whatever life is bringing to happen near us or to us or within us, thus feeling inwardly at peace while we consciously and freely accept the turns of life as they come our way. And then "to us there is satisfaction" for the life we lead and the course of events in God's wide world. This is a fundamental trait of Indian character and it is clearly embedded in the language.

The verb "to have" plays a central role in the English language. Apart from its function as an auxiliary verb, it is constantly used with all kind of objects, physical, mental and moral, to express physical possession, mental situation or inward disposition. I have money, I have a house, a car; I have a dog; I have two hands, a mind, a soul; I have breakfast, a drink, a swim; I have fever, indigestion, a cold; I have a feeling, an idea, a plan; I have faith, doubts, hope; I have a conscience, an inferiority complex, an ambition in life; I have a duty, a good time, a success; I have a bad temper, a good nature, a bright future; I have a friend, a brother, a child; I have a problem, a good name, a bad memory; I have a habit, a passion, a fear. No end of it. It is difficult, indeed impossible, to speak or write English for a length of time without using the verb "to have" in one form or another; and to remove the word "to have" entirely from English would convert English into another language.

Once I asked some Gujarati friends who knew English well to tell me how to say "to have" in Gujarati. They blinked. For one thing, there is no verb in Gujarati corresponding to "to have" in English; and for another, they had never realised the lack of it. It is actually a shocking discovery, and a most enlightening one. This is the single greatest linguistic difference between Gujarati and English – which, in legitimate projection, means between East and West. Gujarati does not have the verb "to have". And it gets along famously without it. Nobody misses it. "I have a brother" becomes "to me there is a brother", "I have an idea" is "to me an idea has come", "I have a good time" means "enjoyment came to me", and for "I have money" we say "near me there is money". This is another planet. We do not "have" or "own" or "possess" money, a book, a pen or any material object, but these things just happen to be "near me" or "beside me" or "close to me". They are there. Much less can we say that I "have" a brother as though I owned him, or that I "have" two hands as though they were a piece of property I could lock up in a safe, or that I "have" a feeling as though I manufactured it. All these things, again, just "happen" to me or "come" to me or "apply" to me or are "near" me, but I don't have, own or possess any of them in any way.

"To have" is a possessive word, and its over-extensive use in a language denotes a possessive tendency in the character of its users. Western mentality does give importance to material possessions as a measure of success in life and a means to enjoy it, while the Indian way of life is based on detachment and renunciation. The expression "near me there is money", which looks so awkward in English, sounds perfectly natural in Gujarati, and as such is used constantly in daily language without anybody paying attention to its hidden significance. It comes in very handy when one wants to refuse politely a petition for money at a particular moment. "Sorry, near me there is nothing." Easier to say than "I have nothing". We should not exaggerate, of course, and people can be greedy or detached both in the East and in the West, but there is a basic attitude and a moral value that makes the West more possessive and the East more detached in tradition, behaviour, doctrine and spirituality.

During a number of days I had observed early in the morning in a narrow street in the old city of Ahmedabad "within the walls" a woman who sold *datan,* that is the freshly cut short thin branch of the *neem* tree that is used in traditional homes as a throw-away toothbrush (a third-world luxury!) for the daily toilette as first body duty on getting up every morning. She would sit on the ground before her neatly arranged bundle of equal parallel sticks to be sold for a few cents to early customers who came down in their night suites to gather the sticks for the morning ritual. One day I observed that it was still early and the old woman had almost sold all her sticks. I stopped in front of her and told her cheerfully: "You are lucky today, grandma. You have already sold all your sticks and you have still time to fetch another load and earn double money today." She looked up to me with non-comprehending wonderment and answered me: "And what do I want double money for? I have already my earnings today, and tomorrow I'll get tomorrow's earnings, God willing. Why should I want more?" By then she had sold her last items, so she folded back the cloth she had spread on the ground, got up and went gently away. Detachment *is* a moral value in India. And that attitude is reflected – and helped – by the language.

When Pandit Nehru paid an official visit to the United States as Prime Minister of India in 1949, President Truman arranged a banquet for him at which some of the wealthiest citizens of America had been invited with a view to solicit their collaboration with development programmes in India. Nehru later narrated the experience and his reaction to it. President Truman, who was seated by his side at the banquet, went quietly pointing out each guest and telling Nehru in a low voice: "This man is worth so many million dollars, that one there is worth so many millions, the next one is worth so many...", and so all down the line. Nehru was horrified. He knew English well, and was conversant with the expression "worth so much" as meaning "has so much money", but even so he was shocked and denounced the irresponsibility of the English language that permits saying that a person is "worth" what he or she "possesses". Personalities measured in money.

Another linguistic insight of Pandit Nehru's in his classic book The Discovery of India is his remark on the significance of the fact that one of the words that English has borrowed from Hindi (together with *"pukka"* or *"pundit"* or *"punkah"*) is the verb "to loot". Apparently the British in India had used the word often.

FAST FOOD

The English language is partial to the verb "to run". Apart from the act of bodily running, it is used for a number of more or less related activities which occupy full columns in any standard dictionary. To run a business, to run for an election, to run a fever, to run into debt, to run short of paper, to run a test, to run out of matches, to run through a list, to run other peoples' lives for them. The Gujarati language is equally partial to the verb "to sit down". We say, spring has sat down, this problem does not sit down, the building sat down (collapsed), the flower has sat down (on the tree), the paint has sat down (dried up), the artist's hand has sat down (on the trade's instruments), the market sits down, our cheeks sit down (with hunger), our chest sits down (with fear), we sit down to eat, to pray, to cry, to sing, and finally we literally "sit down to die". It would seem that the West runs while the East sits down. Again, there is no question of passivity or laziness, but of different outlooks on life. It is not only that India is a warm country while England is cool, but that life runs (or sits down?) to a different rhythm in different places.

The belief or no belief in reincarnation, which I knowingly mentioned at the beginning of the book, influences attitudes and behaviours and the whole life. The westerner, having in general only one life, is always in a hurry to make the best of it, to get the most out of every minute of it (time is money), to crowd into one single incarnation all that a human person has to achieve in that privileged position, to pile up in a short lifetime merits for a whole eternity; while the easterner has plenty of chances (the celebrated *lakh-choriasi* or 8.400.000 births by the last count) to gain merit and polish up rough edges, and therefore can take things easy and relax while on their way to final liberation. We run (again!) to different clocks.

Shortly after my arrival in India I had to undertake a train journey, and I went well in time to the railway station and waited on the platform. There I noticed some disturbance among a group of passengers in holiday clothes, I paid attention to what they were saying, and little by little I tried to unravel their situation which was quite new to me. A wedding party had booked a railway carriage to be attached to a goods train that would take eight hours to reach their destination stopping at all stations. The station master was at the moment explaining to the merry travellers that, as the goods train had been delayed and would not come till the next day, he was proceeding to hitch their carriage to a fast train that would reach their station in four hours without stopping anywhere in between. I felt they were lucky to go twice as fast for the same price, but they did not seem to see it that way. They were protesting. I could not understand why, and it took me some time to realise the point of their protest. They were indignant and kept telling each other and the station master in their anger: "We have paid to be for eight hours in the train; and they want to let us only four? We are entitled to stop at every station; and they want to take us in a hurry like lightning? This is cheating! Either they put us in our proper train or they give us our money back. Do they think that because we are villagers they can fool us any way they like?" I was dumbfounded. In a way they were right. What was the use of arriving for the feast four hours early? They were looking forward to their train journey and their talking and singing and eating and enjoying the train festival together. That was already part of the wedding feast. Let no one spoil the merrymaking. I smiled and boarded my train. It was a fast train.

In my teaching days at College I was lucky enough to accompany a students' holiday tour to Kashmir one year in summer in the happy days of that beautiful, haunting, long-suffering land. The long journey north by train and by bus, the icy river in Pahelgam, the mystic cave of Amarnath, the snow (first snow for all my Ahmedabad students in their life) at Khilanmarg, the panoramic Himalayan view from Gulmarg, the Moghul Gardens, Shalimar, Nishat, Chasma-Shahi in Shrinagar, the house boat on the Dal Lake, the Chinar trees all round. And then the river Jhelum with its seven bridges which bring luck to all those who steer their way under them in the continuous flow of the waters in a *shikara,* the slow moving flat boat accommodating six persons, guided along the gentle current of the river by a single oarsman with a long pole which he wields with skill on the right and the left side of the boat alternately to keep it going straight. I was in one of the *shikaras* sharing its wooden side benches with students who kept singing film songs and playing *antkadi* linking the end of a song with the beginning of another in an endless succession of fun-generating lyrics. It takes the best part of a long afternoon to go under the seven bridges in the traditional, contemplative, liturgical way as we were doing. But then we saw a sight. Something like a whirlwind was coming along the river from behind us and was overtaking us. We stood still. Yes, it was a *shikara,* but this time there was a single passenger standing in the middle of the boat while six oarsmen, three on each side, propelled the boat at a fast pace and he stood upright and kept urging them to speed with American sounding interjections while the oarsmen smiled and laughed out their enjoyment at their new job. Several cameras were hanging from the man's neck and shoulders, and he would take now one now the other for quick snaps of the surroundings. He also snapped us. We understood. He was a tourist who had consulted his guide book, had learned about the seven bridges and had decided "to do them" as the expression goes, taking pictures all along to show his friends back home and to prove to himself and to the world that he had "done" the bridges. We continued with our songs and our pace. We had seen a *shikara* turned into a powerboat. We do follow different timetables.

It could not be otherwise. The westerner shoots along an arrow, the arrow of time, a straight line, a bullet's trajectory, a vector, while the easterner follows the *kala-chakra* or wheel of time, the *ouroboros* or serpent biting its tail, the cycle of creation-conservation-destruction to start all over again at the end as the perfect circle round the cosmic dance of the Nataraj or King of Dance in eternal performance. The circle is round and undivided. There is not even direction, no right to left, no up and down, no beginning or end as the circle is itself however it is placed. In fact, in Gujarati we use the same word *(agal)* to say "before" and to say "after". This sounds utterly impossible to a westerner, but it is true. The sentences "that point came before", and "that will come later" are constructed with the same word *agal,* and it is only the tense in the verb that clears the ambiguity. It was quite confusing to me when I was learning Gujarati and I could never quite make out from the teacher's answer whether a particular lesson had already come *before* or was due to come *later*. It was just *agal.* Thank you.

The word for time is *kal,* and its ablative *kale,* again, can equally mean "yesterday" or "tomorrow" depending on the context. Quite a situation again. The "time that came" was obviously yesterday, and "the time that will come" is tomorrow. But the "time" is the same. *Kal.* The eternal circle. As it goes round and round, every tomorrow becomes yesterday and every yesterday becomes tomorrow. If you go round a circle, point A comes before point B, but if you keep going round, point A will come again *after* point B. So, "before" and "after" mean very much the same thing. We do march to the beat of a different drummer. Punctuality, haste, time saving, an eye on the watch and a calendar on the table is the attitude on one side, while peace, tranquillity, informality, relaxation and playfulness form the other. Both attitudes have advantages. And both have disadvantages.

The West has given us fast food. Fortunately, the West itself, this time Europe as against America, has also invented "slow food" ("Slow Food Movement", Bra, Italy as a counterattack on McDonald's) to rescue the healthy habit of leisurely enjoying good food in good company with good cooking in unhurried restaurants. In India we didn't have the name but we had the art all the time. Quiet meals. Quietly prepared at home with care and love. The best part of the day in the home goes in detailed preparations from buying fresh vegetables in the daily morning bargain of the street market to airing them, cleaning them, washing them, cutting them, boiling them at their different times, adding the spices, presenting them, serving them on the predetermined spots of the awaiting *thali* (wide metal dish) among pickles and salad and hot *dal* and cold curds round a waiting space in the middle for the steaming white rice at the end, creating a meal offering to satisfy gods and humans in the first need and greatest pleasure of all who share in it. Then every flat bread or *rotli* has to be kneaded lovingly, individually, professionally to its round perfection, toasted to brown specs on the hotplate on both sides and anointed with *ghee* while the guests, who are an incarnation of God himself, wait with patient eagerness for the supreme moment of the blessing of food in the daily worship of human existence on earth. *Bismillah kijie.* This is a Muslim invocation often used to bless a Hindu meal. "Do the beginning in the name of God." Ecumenical banquet.

WRITTEN WITH THE HEART

When I was teaching mathematics at College I invited questions by the students in and out of class. Mathematics is a touchy subject and theorems require proofs and problems solutions. Often a student would approach me, in a corridor outside class or in my room in the students' hostel, with an open book in her hands, a finger on a line in the page and a question on her lips: "Please, explain." Now, this "explain" had also a grammatical sting to its tail. The verb for "explaining" in Gujarati means literally "causing to understand". So the student was asking me to make her understand the question, and that was often more than I could do. The word "to teach" means, by the same token, "to cause to learn", and I am sure I've sometimes spent a whole hour "teaching" mathematics on the blackboard without "making" any of my students "learn" anything. They could always insist saying again, "explain that please", which actually meant "make us understand", a task that was often beyond my powers of explanation, that is, of making people understand. This is the sting of the "causative voice", as verbs in the language have active (I lift), passive (I am lifted) and causative voice (I cause to be lifted). And, once more, language means mentality and words mean attitudes. Make me understand.

Not that my students were in any way lazy or stupid or

waited passively to be told, to be taught, to be enlightened. Not by any means. They were bright and diligent and active and did their homework and prepared their examinations. I asked one of them at the beginning of the course whether he knew we had that year an entirely new subject in the course, Three-Dimension Dynamics Through Vectors, which had been announced as coming with a very tough syllabus. She shrugged her shoulders and said nonchalantly: "I've gone through the whole textbook by myself during the holidays and there's nothing much to it." That was not an empty boast, and her performance at every examination proved her mettle. My experience as a teacher with my students is enough to dispel any misunderstanding or cliché about laziness or carelessness of people in tropical climates. We are not lazy, and our language does not reflect or favour any idleness in any way. What it does signify and help to acquire is peace of mind, balance, tranquillity, detachment.

Maybe it is this detached attitude to life and peaceful equanimity, instead of an aggressively result-oriented success-demanding mental and linguistic approach, that has fostered contemplative spirituality and mystical experiences among the saints of India from Mirabhai to Narsingh Mehta and from Tukaram to Namdev. The Catholic Benedictine monk Henri Le Saux, who became very popular and very much loved in India under the name of Swami Abhishiktananda in Shantivanam Ashram, Tamil Nadu, and who knew well his own Catholic tradition of mysticism from St Teresa of Avila to St John of the Cross, used to say with a touch of mischievous humour that "Western mystics cannot reach ultimate unity with the Absolute..., because they don't know Sanskrit!" Language for contemplation.

Western languages have been shaped by a practical mentality of quick communication and simplified grammar, while oriental languages are more complex in their syntax and more varied in their sentence structure with an attention to number, gender and case that gives them individual reference and precise expression far beyond the abstract generalness of languages like English. An example at hand is the relatively recent birth of the "inclusive language" in common English practice. We welcome, on the one hand, America's achievement to have excogitated ways and turns of speech calculated to transform in our days the English language into an impartial language without gender bias, a feat that has been achieved with much ingenuity and not without some skulduggery, and we are grateful for it as it reflects and fosters equality of women and men in our speech and, given the mutual influence we are emphasising throughout between language and behaviour, can help establish that equality in our times. We hail the reform and willingly implement it.

On the other hand, we respectfully beg to remark that this has been possible because English is a very poor language. The soul of a language is its grammar (witness Panini and Hemchandracharya), and the English language has a pitifully stinted grammar (and, of course, no Panini and no Hemchandracharya in its history). Words are important, but they only make up the body of the language in their inert, isolated, fragmented expression, waiting to be summoned, combined, infused by the rules of grammar and the links of syntax that bring life to them, give them sense, and make them into language. As far as vocabulary is concerned, English is a very rich language, building up its lexicon as it does with words and expressions from Anglo-Saxon as well as Indo-European sources – with a sprinkle of exotic borrowings from ex-colonial lands; but as far as grammar is concerned – and, I repeat, grammar is the soul of the language – the English language is notoriously lacking in substance. English has hardly any genders except for the male-female distinction in the animal kingdom (and a few exceptions like its nostalgic reference to ships as female – an indication, perhaps, of the traditionally tender and chivalrous feelings of British subjects towards the Royal Navy thanks to which Britannia once ruled the waves), it has no declensions, no case endings, very few verbal forms in its voices and tenses, and therefore has readily lent itself to a simplification in favour of the equality of the sexes which, although welcome in its significance, is indicative of its weakness as a language. Such a simplification would just be inconceivable in any of our Indian languages given the richness of their grammar, the variety of masculine-feminine-neuter genders throughout their vocabulary (a headache for learners!), the multiplicity of their personal pronouns, the fact that a word may change its meaning by changing its gender, a feat impossible in English because it has no genders. The same goes for verbal forms. In English, the grammatical expressions to run, I run, you run, we run, they run, I have run, I will run..., are all "run", whereas in Gujarati the verbal root has different endings for each one of those cases. Even more, "I run" in the passive tense is said in different ways in Gujarati if the runner is a woman or the runner is a man. The variety and multiplicity of grammatical forms in Indian languages preclude any attempt at their unification in an "inclusive" pattern. You cannot "include" multiplicity.

We do appreciate the gift of an inclusive language in English and have speedily incorporated its rules and turns of phrase into our daily speech (not without some wonderment and a playful knowing wink at times), but at the same time we humbly and proudly submit that our Indian languages cannot comply with any inclusive language regulations simply because their innate perfection and delicate structure prevent any such simplification.

We like to think that our linguistic difference between masculine and feminine forms can also help appreciate the legitimate differences between the sexes and foster their mutual respect and understanding and appreciating on the basis of an equal syntactic treatment in their rich variety. A "unisex" style does not help bring out the diversity, the complexity, the contrast, and the beauty of the human race. Any Frenchman and Frenchwoman will understand this. *Vive la difference!*

Immigrants, for a start, were often troubled by inferiority feelings when their knowledge of English on arrival was not up to the mark, their pronunciation gave them away, their vocabulary was limited and their turns of phrase often obsolete. We do want to master English and to do honour to a world language in knowledge and in use; but a person whose mother tongue (or at least whose mother's tongue) is an ancient language of deep riches and haunting beauty should never feel any linguistic inferiority complex before anybody in the world. All this is written with the heart.

MOTHERS-IN-LAW

In the West my father's brother is my uncle, my mother's brother is my uncle, my father's sister's husband is my uncle, my mother's sister's husband is my uncle. Four uncles, one word. Uncle. In Gujarati there is a different word for each one of those uncles. *Kaka, mama, fua, masa.* And the corresponding ones for aunties, *kaki, mami, foi, masi.* Life in a joint family brings closer relationships, and different words have to be used for different characters with their shades of meaning and their individual characteristics and special place in the family. A mother's sister's husband is not the same as a father's brother. Obviously. Language, again, uncovers life, and richness in vocabulary points towards richness in relationships. Family life in the East is lived differently from the West, and as family is the basic institution and the primary cell of the human race, it is worthwhile to examine differences and to profit by different experiences. Never with a view to judging or preferring one to the other, but always with the desire of sharing and learning from one another.

For ten years of my almost lifelong stay in Ahmedabad I lived begging for hospitality from house to house as a wandering guest in the inner city of narrow lanes and crowded houses within the ancient walls. This, of course, was only possible in India. I would mount my cycle after my classes at the College, reach the outer wards of the city after half an hour pedalling, knock at a door, and ask for hospitality of board and lodging, eating my meals and sleeping for the night with the family, and shifting in the same way to another house after a week. People knew me from my books and my weekly column in the newspapers, which made the instant relationship possible, but I never knew beforehand the family I was going to lodge with the next week. Not a very standard way of life for anybody in an American city, or anywhere in the world for that matter, but not too strange in India where, again, there is a word to describe that way of life for a monk, *vihar,* and where there is the word there is the house. I was the lucky recipient of that generous hospitality (far from my paying anything for my lodging, I was often offered gifts for giving them the chance of serving me!), and that period of my life marked me for ever linguistically, culturally and emotionally.

My first house was that of a Patel family where grandparents, parents, three married and two unmarried brothers, and an undefined number of small children lived happily together. Joint family. That was a new world for me. Quite different from the nuclear family I had known. Again, we are not judging or comparing or lamenting or exalting anything, but just trying to learn from experience, past and present, in order to assimilate the best values each system represents. A joint family fosters security, protection, identification, tradition, company, help in sickness and care in old age, while the nuclear family favours personal growth, freedom, independence, choice, mobility, initiative. In any case, history keeps forging ahead by modelling homes and shaping relationships, and family life will be what circumstances make it to be in each time and place.

Indian immigrants in America pride themselves on having abolished the institution of the mother-in-law. I tend to agree with them. During my home wanderings I knew a family where the mother-in-law forbad her daughter-in-law to read the newspaper until everybody else in the house had read it; in another, the mother-in-law forbad her daughter-in-law to speak English because she herself didn't know the language; in yet another the mother-in-law forbad the daughter-in-law to laugh and even to smile in her presence. Not that her forbidding presence encouraged any smiles, of course, but just as a measure of control and domination. And, what is much more serious and universal and disturbing is the repeated fact, home after home and joint family after joint family, that whenever there was any disagreement or friction, over big or small matters, between the mother-in-law and the daughter-in-law, the man in the family always – always – sided with his mother against his wife no matter how glaringly the wife would be in the right and the mother in the wrong. Nobody regrets the disappearance of the mother-in-law as an institution – except the mothers-in-law.

Still, there is more to the in-laws that has been suggested so far. In a meeting we had in Ahmedabad to exchange experiences between people who had lived abroad for some time and had come back to India, a lady related this experience with great feeling:

"I lived some years in the USA where I had a teaching job. I was married by then, and my husband was with me in America, but our families were in India. One day an American woman friend happened to call on me at my home and found me weeping. She asked me what was the matter, and I told her I had just received a phone call from India with the sad news that my sister-in-law had passed away, and her death had affected me deeply. She there and then exclaimed with surprise: 'What? Crying for your husband's sister? What's the point of that?' She did not understand our family ties – even with our in-laws. To me a sister-in-law was a sister. To her, apparently, it was nothing. I was shocked."

In this matter we are all learning. Sometimes with pain, with doubt, with reluctance, sometimes with openness, eagerness, wonder, but we are all learning, growing, living, and finding out the multiple ways in which we human beings discover not only new lands but new friends and new ties, and possibly a new family in a new land. It is personal contacts, friendships and family links that provide an ideal meeting ground for understanding, knowing and learning.

First-generation immigrants faced a delicate situation with respect to their parents. They had grown in the protection, the care, the security and the love of the joint family, and so they had acquired the "debt" they had to repay their parents by looking in turn after them in their old age. But they migrated abroad and the "debt" remained unpaid. Still the bond and the love remained. Visits were encouraged, money was sent, needs were provided for, contact was continued, and understanding parents felt happy seeing their children move up in society as they had always wished for them. No guilt should be felt on one side, and no recrimination should be made on the other, as life follows its course and each generation finds its own way along the upward path.

There is much to share, much to learn, much to give and take in the matter of family life with all its delicate and intricate texture in its different forms and its evolving shape. A feature in this experience stands out and that is that Indian immigrants in America are singled out and praised by their American friends for the stability of their marriages and the unity of their extended families. May this continue.

ISSEI, NISEI, AND SANSEI

Marriage also offers the two varieties, roughly corresponding to the joint and to the nuclear family: set up by the families or entered upon by the young people by themselves. Arranged marriage versus love marriage. A situation that for emigrants abroad gets further involved by the increasing variety of choices and possibilities. Here is a letter from a mother in India to her daughter in America:

> "Yesterday we got a letter from Naina Aunty. Her friend's son, a boy of twenty-six, is doing his Ph.D. in Stanford. He is tall, fair and very handsome. His family background is very cultured. Both his parents are lawyers. They are looking for a suitable match for him, and Naina Aunty, who loves you so much, immediately thought of you and mentioned to them that you are also in the States. Now, before losing your temper with me, listen properly. This is just a suggestion. We are not forcing you into a marriage you don't want. But you must keep an open mind. At least meet him. Rather, he will come to the university to meet you. Give your father and me the pleasure of saying, there is someone who will look after our child.
>
> Every day I pray that you will not marry an American. That would be very hard on us. One day you would

bring us an American son-in-law. You know we will accept even that if we have to, but it will make us most unhappy." (Anjana Appachana, Her Mother, p. 7)

In fairness to the institution we have also to present the opposite view, this time from the touching and thought-provoking experience of a well-known and well-respected editor in India, M.V. Kamath. Here is his story:

"Some time in the winter of 1950 I went home to Udupi on leave from my Bombay job as reporter to *The Free Press Journal*, now knowing that I was going to get a stern lecture from father on the importance of marrying before it became 'too late'. My salary was low and was seldom paid on time and, had it not been that I was living with my eldest brother who affectionately accommodated me, I would have been broke most of the time. The thought of marriage was far away from my mind. Living in discreet poverty in some slum on an income that was illusory was not my concept of how to make a happy marriage.

Father did not apparently wish to spoil my vacation right from the start, so he waited until the night before I was to return to Bombay. The family had been told to foregather that night to assist father in getting his recalcitrant son agree to marriage. The moment came.

Dinner over, father, mother, two sisters, a brother, brothers-in-law and others gathered in the spacious portico of the house and innocently I joined them.

Ours was an old-fashioned family. In all the years when father was alive, I don't think I ever had a face-to-face talk with him. For solving any problem I went to my mother. Disobeying father was out of question.

That night in front of the family my father told me that it wasn't 'proper' that I should remain single any longer, that I should show a sense of responsibility, that luckily he had found the ideal girl for me to get married and that all that was necessary was my consent. He gave a glowing account of my would be – and proposed – in-laws, adding that the girl he had found for me to get married to was a 'gem'. Father, apparently, had also told the would be in-laws that my affirmative reply was a foregone conclusion. No one would dare to disobey his father's desire. That was impossible even to think of.

I sat listening in abject fear. Even singly I couldn't afford to rent an apartment for myself. My bank balance was nil. I literally lived from hand to mouth. Asking for a huge dowry was to me disgraceful. My father was in no position to support me either. And I did not want to be a burden on my brother.

But these were not matters of great account to father's old-fashioned ways. One married young because one *had* to marry young. Money would come in time. And when one was young, one learnt to accommodate oneself to one's limitations. The family, of course, was totally supportive of father. But I was unwilling to accept the challenge. I was unwilling to say 'yes' to father and afraid to say 'no'. The matter ended in a stalemate.

The next day I returned to Bombay. Through my brother I conveyed to the family that I was not yet ready for marriage. It broke my father's heart. Not long after he had a heart attack and died. I felt doubly guilty.

Years passed. I grew up, changed jobs, made good

financially, and, as the say, 'rose in the ranks' to become the editor of *The Illustrated Weekly of India*, then the most popular magazine in the country. I was invited to a community gathering to be 'honoured' for the occasion. Among the many who had gathered to honour me was an old friend, whom I hadn't seen for years. Noticing my arrival, he came running to me and said: 'Madhav, what a pleasure to see you after all there years. Come, I want to introduce you to your wife!'

I thought he was mixing up words in his excitement. I said: 'I beg your pardon. You mean *your* wife?' Smiling broadly and somewhat mischievously he said: 'Yes, no, but doesn't matter. She is your wife!'

By then a beautiful and charming woman had joined us who greeted me warmly with a *namaskar*. She, too, was smiling broadly. I had never met her before and I respectfully greeted her.

'Your wife, Madhav', said my friend. Totally at a loss to know what was going on, I said: 'What's the joke? I don't get you.' It was then that my friend explained that this was the girl I was supposed to marry but hadn't. She now was his wife.

It was an embarrassing moment. Standing next to me was one of the loveliest women I had ever known, not only just beautiful, but from what I could gather warm-hearted and noble. At that point in time I wished earth would open before me and receive me in her arms.

'Laxmi (name changed)', I said to her, 'What a lucky girl you are! Married to such a fine man. My congratulations to you. Imagine what trauma you would have had to undergo marrying an impecunious reporter as myself!'

We all had a good laugh. But I am afraid I blushed deeply. And romantic that I am, I thought perhaps I should have obeyed my father's intentions like any good son!" (M.V. Kamath, A Journalist at Large, Jaico, Mumbai 2006, p. 172)

The humour of the situation softens its pathos. The reporter, later posted for years in Washington, married an American. Called back to India to 'rise in the ranks' as he has said, his American wife accompanied him willingly, only to find soon that climate and circumstances did not suit her, and she went back.

Inter-culture marriage has to be looked into in the context of immigration where it is called to play a fundamental though not yet sufficiently explored role. The instinctive choice for a marriage partner among first immigrants was for a person of the same country, origin, society, language, caste, religion, and we have seen testimonies of the parents' choices just now. In early immigration days, newspapers in India began carrying long columns of advertisements of marriageable youths settled in America who were coming for a short holiday to India where they invited applications from young ladies ready to cross the seas and settle in a new land with bright prospects and all facilities. The scheme worked, and festive weddings were celebrated in hastily worked out horoscope-friendly auspicious days (often with a bribe to condescending planets), and happy families increased the numbers of residents abroad and strengthened their bonds among themselves. That was the ideal marriage. But things are changing fast.

Canadian television ecological star, Japanese-Canadian David Suzuki, reflects significantly on the marriage relationships within his own family and the change they have undergone within three generations, giving us along the way very valuable hints on immigrants' family situations, whether they be Issei, Nisei, or Sansei (explanation follows).

"My maternal and paternal grandparents emigrated to Canada, less because they wanted to make a new life than because in Japan they were locked into extreme poverty. Japan was their home, and their intent was to return to it when they had made their fortune. But it was a journey to a distant land with no assurances they would ever return. After my birth, my father's parents never went back to Japan, and my mother's parents returned only after World War II, disillusioned by their treatment in Canada. They went back to Hiroshima, and both were dead in less that a year.

My father and mother were born in Vancouver in 1909 and 1910 respectively, and survived the trauma of the Great Depression thanks to hard work and a strong extended family, which was held together by economic necessity and the forces of racism in British Columbia at the time. Even though their social lives revolved around family and other Japanese, however, my parents felt themselves fully Canadian." (David Suzuki, The Autobiography, Allen & Unwin, Sydney 2006, p. 3)

"Buffered from the world by my parents, I didn't know Japan had attacked Pearl Harbor in Hawaii on December 7, 1941, and I didn't sense any fear or consternation in Mom or Dad. The treachery implicit in Japan's 'sneak attack' against the United States Navy and the terrible war that followed threw my family and some twenty thousand other Japanese Canadians into a turbulent sequence of events, beginning with our deprivation of all rights of citizenship. The evacuation of Japanese Canadians from the coast of British Columbia and their incarceration in internment camps generated enormous resentment within the community. In my teen years, my identity was based on the consciousness that in the eyes of white Canadians, I was Japanese first, Canadian second. All my life as an adult, my drive to do well has been motivated by the desire to demonstrate to my fellow Canadians that my family and I had not deserved to be treated as we were." (p. 14)

"Of course, Japanese Canadians still held strong ties to Japan. The Japanese who came to Canada (called Issei, or first generation) still had family and friends back in the 'old country'. Like all immigrant people, the first generation of Japanese-heritage kids born in Canada (called Nisei, or second generation) had to grow up without grandparents or an extended family here. This was a sharp break from traditional values surrounding family and elders, and Issei were especially concerned about the loss of those values. As a Sansei (third generation) born of Canadian-born parents, I did have grandparents living in Vancouver and saw them regularly, but, being unilingual, I was almost cut off from them. My life in the internment camp was my first experience of alienation and isolation, and it gave me a lifelong sense of being an outsider. Soon after Pearl Harbor, my father had volunteered to go to that road camp where Japanese Canadians were helping to build the Trans-Canada Highway. He had hoped that by volunteering, he would demonstrate his good intentions, trustworthiness, and willingness to leave his family as hostages to ensure his continued good behaviour, therefore ensuring we would be allowed to remain in Vancouver. But it wasn't to be. I am amazed that somehow my parents, still in their early thirties, were able to shield my sisters and me from the pain, anger, and fear that must have threatened to overwhelm them, as the only country they had ever known branded them enemy aliens who could not be trusted." (16)

"In London (Canada), puberty in a time of straitlaced attitudes towards sex, fear of pregnancy, and 'shotgun marriages' was difficult enough, but as a Japanese Canadian scarred by the war and internment, I had a small potential field of girls to consider. Restricted by my father's edict that I must find a mate who was Japanese, I protested there were too few teenage Japanese girls in all of London, so Dad allowed me to consider dating a Chinese Canadian. 'Dad', I pleaded, 'there are only three Chinese families here and I don't know any of them.' 'Okay, okay', he relented, 'a Native girl is all right.' When I pointed out that there might be other immigrants' reserves on the outskirts of town, but I certainly did not know any Native girls, he added a black girl to the list of acceptables. The only black girl I knew was Annabel Johnson (the writer), and she certainly was not interested in me. 'All right, I'll allow a Jewish girl', he said, grudgingly, having run out of visible minorities. Dad's descending order of potential mates was based on ethnicity and the extent to which he felt the women themselves would have experienced prejudice, but he failed to recognise that he implicitly accepted the stereotypes and limitations of the bigots." (p. 37)

[Suzuki eventually married a British girl, Tara Cullis, settled in Canada.] "When we met, I had told Tara I anticipated her parents would have objections to me because of my race and my age. To my amazement

and everlasting respect, neither of those were issues."
(p. 99)

"Every one of the nine siblings of my parents' families
married Japanese. Today, among dozens of their
children and grandchildren, only my twin sister,
Marcia, is married to a Japanese." (p. 5)

This last bit of information is amazing. International
marriages. Within one generation, marriage patterns seem
to have been radically altered in the Suzuki family. This
doesn't seem to be a general phenomenon all round, but it
does strike a note and announce a development that is fast
overtaking us. First comers spontaneously sought support
from their equals in race and religion, and closely knit
families helped to build up a community. But as generation
succeeds generation, as Issei are succeeded by Nisei, and
Nisei by Sansei, spaces widen up, contacts multiply, and
barriers between groups gently crumble down. So long as
it is the parents who choose marriage partners for their
children, the traditional pattern of marriage within race,
religion, and caste, will be favoured before mixed ventures;
but as the young people, men and women, increasingly
take it upon themselves to find their life partners in open
societies, social conventions are challenged, tastes and
preferences diversify, and customs change. Origin and
religion cease to be an issue, personal choice ignores ancient
traditions, and mixed marriages result. The tendency is on
the increase.

Some marriage counsellors go to the length of saying
that marriage between people of different religions can
be more enriching and even safer than within the same
religion. Here is the explanation. When two Hindus or two
Muslims or two Christians marry, they come from similar
backgrounds, and so they tend to take for granted common

issues, not realising that the same traditions or beliefs can be interpreted differently in different families and by different individuals, and that these different practical interpretations can cause difficulties in the daily life of the new couple. Religion is not discussed, but the same religion can be quite differently interpreted and practiced by two people within it, and these differences will soon show up at home and may generate friction. On the other hand, if bride and bridegroom come from different religious backgrounds, this fact will be in their minds from the beginning, will be mentioned, studied, evaluated, discussed. Each partner will learn from the other partner new doctrines, convictions, practices, and, what can be even more important, each partner will explain to the other their own religious doctrines, convictions, practices, and in the process of doing so, will become clearer in their mind and steadier in their heart about their own religion. Benefit for both.

I knew a young Indian in Spain, born of Hindu parents that left Pakistan at the time of partition to settle in the Canary Islands, who, being and remaining a Hindu, married a Catholic girl. In the process, he learned his catechism, attended mass on Sundays with his wife, and even served at mass, without receiving Holy Communion, of course, but with full mastery of prayers and rubrics. And I know a Catholic couple who married in love and mutual dedication, only soon to experience some friction as the wife insisted on attending mass every Sunday, while the husband, also baptised a Catholic, was not in the habit of visiting churches even on Sundays. They had taken the religious issue for granted to their undoing.

Friction within the same religion. A charming couple of my close acquaintance in India fasted, as many Hindus do, one day in the week. The husband fasted on Wednesdays, and the wife on Saturdays. I, trying to be stupidly helpful, volunteered to suggest that it would be easier for them in the kitchen and in their timetable if they could unify their austerities; but they benevolently smiled and shook their heads. No, it wasn't done. Each fast was prompted by a guru, and the guru's injunctions cannot be altered. There is the story of the prince and princess who married, and on their wedding day the prince confided to the princess that for one half of the month on each month they would have to keep separate nights, as his guru had enjoined on him abstention from sex for the dark fortnight of the lunar month each month for life. The bride, on hearing that, fainted straightaway. When she came back to, the prince, surprised at her marital eagerness, hastened to console her, as they always had the bright fortnight of the month to make up; but then she woefully explained that her own guru had put her under a vow not to have sex during the bright fortnight of the lunar month every month for life. That wiped out their calendar for them. For life they kept a naked sword in bed between them as they honoured their guru. It was the same guru for both, of course, with a rather black sense of humour. To have the same guru can be dangerous at times.

These are only indications of the manifold paths human relations are taking as we go on discovering what we all thought had long been discovered, and exploring anew the inexhaustible riches of the human being in person and in family. Without influencing tastes or forestalling choices, it is clear that inter-culture marriages will help mutual understanding, will bring peoples and religions closer together, will become in time indistinguishable as the current of life sweeps through continents and shapes history.

After Issei comes Sensei, and after Sensei comes Sansei.

What comes after Sansei?

THE RED THREAD

A special relationship in the Indian family is that between brother and sister. Brother's Day is not a very popular date worldwide, but it is fervently observed in India, and that not once but twice in the year. The first date is none other than the first day after New Year, which is also the last of the five-day festival of Diwali with which India bids farewell to the old year and ushers in the new. I will here go briefly through the festivities to focus the feast of the Brother and Sister, and to give a glimpse of a field in which we have also much to share, to learn, and to teach: religious and cultural festivals in our traditions. Indian families settled abroad unfailingly celebrate Diwali, and it is good for them to revise the meaning of their feast, and for us all to share in their customs.

The festival accompanies the new moon in her darkest days to be led by her in her growing phase towards the new light of the new year. The first day is *Dhanteras,* or Rich Thirteenth, the thirteenth day in the dark fortnight of the moon, in honour of Lakshmi, goddess of wealth and of the tools we create it with. The farmer in that day worships their bullocks and plough, the carpenter their hammer and saw, the cook their pots and pans, and the shopkeeper their account books. For us this is the day to offer *puja* (worship) to our computer, to garland it, wave the light of auspicious candles all round its screen, mark it on the centre of the frame with the red turmeric spot, join hands before it, and bow gently after caressing the monitor, the CPU, the keyboard and the mouse in loving and respectful gesture. It is the best antivirus for the whole year.

The second day is *Kalichaudas,* Dark Fourteenth, and remembers Yama, the god of death. It integrates the dark side of things into the totality of existence, obstacles into success, death into life, thus allaying suffering and softening setbacks. Yama is The Supreme Guest, who, as a true guest *(a-tithi)* arrives without a date *(tithi),* and for whose unexpected coming we have prepared ourselves by welcoming all the guests that ever arrived at our door without announcing themselves as well as all the troubles that overtook us in our lives without expecting them. Hospitality to all people and acceptance of all happenings is a treasured and meaningful value at the heart of Indian spirituality.

Diwali itself is the centre of the feast. The Row of Lights. *Deepawali.* The path through the forest that loving devotees lit up for Rama and Sita as they returned from exile to their people and their throne. A small earthen lamp can light up a whole continent when united to millions like it along the length and breadth of the land. Dots of light that design the profile of India in the night of nights. The auspicious moment to look back on our past life to make sense of its trajectory, and to visualise the future to set our sights. All to the joyful accompaniment of the crackers and rockets that keep alive the night.

Then follows the New Year proper, *Nutan Varsh.* The day of greetings. Everybody to meet everybody. Hands palm to palm together, head bowed, and the New Year traditional greeting on one's joyful lips: *Sal mubarak!* Linguistically *sal* (year) is Farsi, and *mubarak* (blessed) is Arabic, and this is the formula used by all, Hindus and Muslims, Jains and Parsis, Sikhs or Christians in a practical show of verbal ecumenism that reminds us that we all are one before life's events and nature's cycles. The many years I lived in Ahmedabad I spent the whole of this day on my cycle going from house to house, greeting friends, smiling at faces, tasting sweets, drinking tea, renewing acquaintances, caressing streets and loving the city. It was a day of universal friendship and it should remain ever more so.

The last day is Brother's Day. *Bhaibij* or Brother on the Second. The second day of the first new moon in the new year. It again has to do with Yama, the god of death. He went on that day to his twin sister, Yamuna's house. She fed him an exquisite meal, and asked him for the blessing she had a right to ask for after the feast: "Promise me that any brother who on this day may go to eat his meal at his sister's house will not die an untimely death." "*Tathastu*", said The God of Death obligingly, which means "let it be so", and the custom was born. On this day any man with a sister will go to her house, eat the meal prepared by her, and receive the blessing of Yama's protection. A feast to seal the loveliest of loves on earth, the love between brother and sister.

If the brother cannot go to eat that day to his sister's place, there is still the other festival I've mentioned for him. *Rakshabandhan* or The Tying of the Protective Thread. This is one of the loveliest days in India. I was on that day one year, during my pilgrimage from house to house I mentioned above, housing with a family where there was one boy and three sisters, all of College age. In the morning, as I sat down working at my writings, and the boy of the house was reading something by my side, we saw his big sister coming. We knew the rite. We stood up, the girl approached her brother, he extended his right hand, she then tied round his right wrist a red thread she had ready, and touched his feet. The boy touched her head lightly, and then gave her the gift he had prepared for her, a new, crisp banknote. We three felt deeply and said nothing. But then I had noticed the girl had brought one more red thread with her. She looked at me. I guessed. I, too, was her brother. I extended my right hand. She tied the thread and touched my feet. I blessed her. Then I smiled: "I have nothing for you, Rupa." She said: "Then I'll ask for something. Promise you will keep the thread till Dassera." I knew and I said: "I promise." On Brother's Day in the streets one can see red threads on the wrists of all fortunate men who have a sister. But most remove it at the end of the day. The old custom, however, little known and less observed, bids the brother keep the thread till the festival of Dassera, a couple of months away, when it is untied and burned. I kept my promise, and so I kept my thread on my wrist. So when the next day after Brother's Day I faced my mathematics class at College and extended my right hand to begin writing on the blackboard, the red thread shone on my wrist, and a subdued murmur swept through the class. Who can have tied him the thread? I kept my secret. Two months later, on the day of Dassera, the day of Rama's triumph over Ravana, when Good triumphs over Evil, when a long war is ended, when a continent rejoices and time becomes timeless, I loosened the thread, brought it to my forehead, burned it in reverence. But its memory stays with me for ever.

The slender red thread has the advantage that it can be sent by mail. This has to be done in time so that it can be worn on its auspicious day. But it can reach any corner in any continent, and so the family festival of sisterly love can be kept alive wherever a girl from India has a brother, remembers him, and loves him. The thread embodies a double blessing. The brother, on accepting it, binds himself to defend and protect his sister in the troubled world into which she is stepping. When Queen Karmavati of Mewar was attacked by Sultan Bahadur Shah, she sent the red thread to Emperor Humayun who chivalrously hastened to come with his army to help his "sister" in royalty and save her kingdom. Brother protects sister. In this case a Moghul Emperor helps a Hindu Queen. And then, also, the sister protects the brother. The thread she ties to his wrist is like the seal of the king on his messenger, that identifies him, defends him, proclaims to all that this is the king's man and whoever touches him touches the king. So he, too, is safe through his sister's blessing in his own troubled world. That is the power of a bit of red thread and of the hoary tradition hidden in it.

One year, on the day after *Rakshabandhan,* all the daily papers in Ahmedabad brought out a telling photograph on their first page. The social work society *Sadvichar Samiti* had organised the previous day a Rakshabandhan Programme in the Sabarmati Jail. Several city ladies had gone to the jail and had tied to inmates the read thread, thus calling them "brothers" whatever the situation that had confined them within walls. One of the ladies had tied the thread to the man who had murdered her own husband and had been convicted for the crime that had made her a widow. She was calling him brother. Forgiveness, tears, repentance, the highest love of brother and sister brought to bear on the lowest deed of man at his worst. A festival can have its meaning and can have its strength. We'll do well to keep it throughout the world and to gently explain to others the small red thread on our wrist. Brothers Day. Sisters Day. In India we call all women "sisters".

MANGAL

Once the well-known Gujarati writer and friend, Ishwar Petlikar, interviewed me for the daily *Sandesh* in Ahmedabad, and his first question was: "You have lived so many years in India in close contact with its people. What is the most important thing India has given you?" I answered him that India had enlarged my own concept of God. The answer was not flying out at a tangent to avoid the issue, but coming right to the point, as the concept we have of God is what rules our lives. "Tell me which God you worship and I will tell you who you are." I just mention a trait.

Western theologians of both sexes are getting a little concerned now-a-days about the masculinity of God. God is neither man nor woman, simply has no sex, but in the west we have conceived him as Father, and his incarnation is a man, Jesus. In Hinduism the three persons of the Hindu Trinity, Brahma-Vishnu-Shiva have their respective wives Saraswati-Lakshmi-Parvati, and Saraswati is as much God as Brahma, Lakshmi as Vishnu, and Parvati as Shiva. Six divine persons forming one only God, or rather three persons, each of them made up by a masculine-feminine couple. And when the second person of the Hindu Trinity (coincidentally), Vishnu, becomes man in Krishna, Lakshmi becomes a woman in Radha, who is Shri Krishna's wife, and she is as much an incarnation of the divinity as he is. That inclusion of the feminine in the concept of God in the Hindu faith brings theology, liturgy, and popular devotion to life. It also satisfies a trend in present day mentality. The quest for equality between the sexes at the highest level.

We even find the representation in art of *Ardha-nari-ishwar*, that is "Half-woman-god" in which one side of the image is masculine and the other feminine, thus uniting both sexes in one divinity. In this, Indian religious thought has anticipated the latest trends in Western theologies with their belated efforts to place the concept of God beyond gender after having conceived it for centuries as exclusively masculine. Some Christians are heard today to begin the Lord's Prayer saying "Father-Mother in heaven" instead of "Our Father in heaven", the devotion to Mary is a cherished trait of Catholic Christianity, and versions of the Bible in inclusive English have been proposed. The standard joke is repeated of the astronaut who returns to earth after being in orbit and walking in space, and is asked:

-   Have you met God up there?
-   Yes, of course.
-   Could you give us a description of what you saw?
-   Well, yes. She is black.

In India Shri Krishna's name means precisely "Black", "The Dark One", with all his beauty and charm and originality; and the gender of the divinity can be expressed in Hinduism, as we have seen, in either man or woman, so that we have anticipated, in a way, the astronaut's discovery in colour and gender. Beyond joke or legend, now, these are conceptual highlights in a vital and delicate area which is the very concept of God. As our relationship with God will depend on the concept we have of him (or her), and our relationship with God influences all our life and behaviour, these conceptions are significant and far-reaching in the religious search of humankind.

On the other hand, placing man and woman on the same level with reference to the concept of God in Hindu tradition has not, unfortunately, had its counterpart in the honouring, valuing and placing woman on an equal ground with man in social life and daily relationship. Woman has been made subservient to man, and wife to husband, and a son has traditionally been preferred to a daughter. This is sad. The need for a son comes from the desire to perpetuate one's name (for the father), to lengthen the family tree, to have an heir, to ensure help and continuity in business, to prove one's virility, to boast before society of having a complete family as it should be, and finally to have the son light one's funeral pyre in the last rite that will ensure a happy rebirth and that only a son can perform. More practically, a son in the joint family is needed to bring home in time a bride who will take over all the home duties, will serve her parents-in-law in all their needs, will make sure that they are properly looked after at home throughout their lives till they die. As for the girl, on the contrary, she will not remain at home; a suitable partner will have to be found for her and a substantial dowry paid to ensure her acceptance in the new home that will be hers for life with her in-laws. And here comes the point. The girl will not serve her own family in which she is born, she will not be an asset to her own people, will have to be trained, educated, provided with saris and gold to be sent outside, will not help her parents in their old age, but will be transferred to another home, God knows where, and will be lost to her people in her presence and her assistance. She belongs elsewhere. This tends to make a son's birth wanted and a girl's birth unwanted, chiefly if it is the first child. This is regrettable. It is the greatest single harm the practice of the joint family brings to society. As the son remains in it while the daughter leaves, a son is treasured and a daughter is less prized. This concept is tied to the joint family practice and will weaken with it.

A Gujarati film that run for months to full audiences had the story and the title of *Parki Thapan*. That means "Foreign Capital", "Outside Investment", "Someone Else's Gain". That is what the girl in the family is, and that is the way she is treated. Someone else's gain. *Parki Thapan*. A dismal expression. Once a man in a rather high social position became a father to his eagerly expected first child. I learned about it and, as I knew him personally, I phoned to congratulate him. He sounded almost apologetic in his response: "It's a girl. That will have to do." I was saddened.

As a redeeming feature, a girl in the family is traditionally considered something *mangal,* and that is such a beautiful word that it almost makes up by itself for all the unfair discrimination against the fair sex. *Mangal* is an untranslatable word in its depth, its meaning, its sound, its ring, its aura, its freshness, its blessing. It is religious, mystical, familiar, emotional. English language lacks the term. The dictionary gives auspicious, beneficial, favouring, blessing. All that is fine, but *mangal* is much more than that and at the same time something entirely different from all that in its tradition, its memories, its occasions, its tenderness, its bliss. Its very pronunciation is an experience by itself. *Mangal.* It cleans the air and quickens the heart. *Mangal.* Signal example of the fact that each language has treasures exclusive to itself and gems of sense and feeling that bear no translation and stand as pools of light and living waters in the drab wasteland of meanings and synonyms. *Mangal.* That is what the girl is in the family. Woman is always and everywhere something *mangal.* And that is a romance by itself.

BLACK IS BEAUTIFUL

Another point where we in India are not quite consistent between theory and practice with gods and humans is the matter of colour. The goddess Durga Mata is *Kali* which means "black" as she truly and shiningly is in all her representations, and Shri Krishna is *Shyamsundar*, which is literally a centuries-old anticipation in Sanskrit of the contemporary slogan in English, "Black Is Beautiful", as *"shyam"* means "dark" and *"sundar"* means "beautiful". Yet, the slogan is applied only to gods, and the colour that is worshiped in the divinity is regretted in its worshippers. A dark skin is still a liability at the time of planning marriage or applying for a job, a cloud in the family, a hindrance in social relations, and a stubborn obstacle to self-esteem ever. Languages are learned when immigrants proceed to distant lands, pronunciation is polished with time, slang is mastered, manners are adopted, table etiquette is acquired, even names are anglisised if need be, differences are erased and nothing would mark out a second or third generation immigrant from the rest of their fellows in speech and gesture or accent or hair style. Nothing except skin. Shades of skin. Colour. The brown shadow. The cloud.

The sun of India extends its golden touch through spaces and oceans, through births and ages, through clouds and climates, through dynasties and generations, and persists in reminding the Indian, who was already born far from India and has perhaps never been there, of their land of origin, of their ethnic identity, of their relationship to the soil in their body and in their skin, of their monsoons and their droughts, of their rain and their sun. Colour travels with the person and is part of their conscience in themselves and their identity before others. Colour is an issue in many societies today. Whitening creams are profusely offered in the modern cosmetic fashion markets, and are widely used by women and men around the world. White – unfairly, unjustly, preposterously, absurdly, unhappily and regretfully in contrast to black – continues to be and mean pre-eminently beautiful. The adjective "fair" in English means both "pale in skin colour" and "beautiful". Unfair synonyms.

I came to know a bright young Indian student well on his way to becoming a seasoned scientist in the United States, who eventually abandoned his bright chances there and came back to India to a lesser future simply because he was too dark, had been the object of some jokes in poor taste on account of his appearance, and the exaggerated colour complex that grew from that unfortunate experience within him made it unpleasant for him to remain in less friendly surroundings. A true colour victim.

I also knew a girl with all the bright qualities a young woman can desire, as she was educated, intelligent, tall and good-looking, and proceeded from a much respected family, who, in spite of all that, thought poorly of herself, derided herself, withdrew visibly before others, and systematically declined the attention she obviously deserved. What was wrong with her? I learned it in a painful unburdening confidence later. Her mother had once told her in an unguarded moment of parental anger in her childhood when she was old enough to understand the taunt and too young still to be unable to protect her own tender feelings from the meanness of the unseemly attack: "You'll never get anywhere in life! You are black! You're the burden on my back! Nobody will marry you!" That single supposed blemish was enough to overshadow all the splendid qualities that girl possessed all round. It took a good deal of gentleness, persuasion, therapy, and simple getting back to reality to get her to accept herself as she was and to realise her own value. She even laughed when I invited her to recite the opening lines of The Song of Songs in the Old Testament:

> "I am dark but lovely,
> daughters of Jerusalem,
> like the tents of Kedar
> or the tent curtains of Shalmah.
>
> Do not look down on me;
> dark of hue I may be
> because I was scorched by the sun,
> when my mother's sons were displeased with me
> and sent me to watch over the vineyards under the
> sun." Song of Songs 1:5-6)

An Indian in America went to spend a couple of months in India. When he came back, his friends in America told him: "You've come back darker." They were colour-conscious. Over-sensitive. Perhaps also a little jealous that their friend had enjoyed a holiday home and they wanted to lower his euphoria after it. The sun is still the protagonist.

This is a quotation from Anurag Mathur in the book I've mentioned some pages back:

> "Gopal had never really thought of himself as being any particular colour while in India. Here in America it defined nearly every moment of his life. Nor was he

used to receiving so much attention and he certainly didn't enjoy it, particularly because it arose from curiosity rather than approval. Yet he was helpless at blending with the others. Often when he walked into a room he felt that his skin had burst into flames. It was as though so many glances locking on to him sparked a kind of spontaneous combustion. He sensed a few people shrink, others become too friendly, nobody was normal.

His entire life in India had become irrelevant and meant nothing. Not his own achievements, not his family's affluence, everything was beyond the curtain of mirrors with which America bounded itself. Nothing beyond mattered. Here he had to re-create himself, but the basic building block of his new persona was his colour. No matter what he achieved, or however respected he became in the classroom, the moment he stepped outside, his colour came and wrapped itself around him like a clown's clothes that had been hanging outside, waiting for him. In the classroom itself though, he felt a sense of being de-coloured; the better he did, the less alien and awkward he felt. He revelled in the sense of attracting respect. But once outside, he constantly felt as though nature had constructed him badly." (p. 89)

Richard Rodriguez is a Mexican immigrant in the United States who has feelingly and explicitly written about his own experience in this delicate matter. His story is touching:

"Our parents instructed us, their four children, to say simply 'We are Mexicans' when we were asked about our country of origin, which was often. They made fun of those Mexican-Americans who had a fairer skin and passed themselves as Spaniards. My parents would have never denied their origin. I never denied it either, and I mechanically introduced myself as Mexican to all strangers.

My elder sister never spoke to me about the colour of her skin when she was a child. But I understood that her dark skin was a burden for her. She had suffered because she was 'black'. When she came back home, while still at primary school, white children run after her, pushed her and tripped her. In secondary school she had to compete against the other girls for the attention of the boys, and her dark skin was a handicap. In the university she felt frightened and threatened when dark-skinned students form Turkey or India found her attractive. She only spoke to me of her dark-skin complex when she was married, and one day calmly told me her relief at the fact that her three children had fair skin.

This is the type of commentary women in my family would often make. When I was small, I often played in the kitchen and I remember hearing my aunties speak about their joy at having fair children. It was one of their favourite topics of conversation: the fear to have dark-skinned children. One of my aunties prescribed the remedy: large doses of castor oil during the last weeks of pregnancy. Infants born with a dark skin would be treated with a facial mixture of white of egg and concentrated lemon juice. (In my case, the remedy did not work.)

There was even a kind of black humour in this matter. One of my uncles called his wife 'black', but he did it with a loving smile and great tenderness. One of my aunties called her darkest child 'my ugly one' with the same love while she caressed and kissed him. And then they all at times spoke of white skinned people in a derogatory way, saying that the 'gringos' had a 'dough' face and should bask a little in the sun in order not to look like corpses.

In my own experience I felt shame and inferiority because of my dark skin. I grew up convinced that I was ugly. One night, when I must have been eleven or twelve, I locked myself in the bathing room and looked at my reflection in the mirror. I opened the tap, soaked my arms, soaped them, took my father's razor and slowly, deliberately, firmly, placed the blade on my skin, pressed down as much as I could without cutting myself and waved it up and down my skin to see if I somehow could diminish the darkness of my skin. All that I got, of course, was that I shaved the hairs on my arms. That way I found out that the darkness would not disappear. It was there, firmly embedded in the cells of my own skin.

During my adolescence I felt like a marked man. I was obsessed by the colour of my skin. I must have been twelve or fourteen when in drawing class we were asked to draw our self-portrait. I just could not bring myself to colour my face as it was in reality. I identified myself in group photos at once by the colour of my skin. I was ashamed of my body. I wanted to forget I had a body because my body was black." (Ricardo Rodriguez, Hunger of Memory, Megazul, Madrid 1994, p. 132, 142)

Colour bar is as much or even more the way the coloured persons see themselves as the way the others see them. It was another Mexican immigrant, this one a Catholic priest in Madrid, who told me one day: "I cannot bear the way people look at me. In the street, in the office, in shops, in the bus. They look and look and stare and stare. I'm not that dark either, just a shade over them, but that is enough for them to discriminate me and banish me with their looks. I cannot bear it. I'm going back to my country." Which he did. But then I told about this incident to another Mexican immigrant of my close acquaintance and friendship, and he shrugged his shoulders unconcerned and spoke with a contented spontaneity that carried conviction: "That is *his* problem. I also come from Mexico and I also have a tint to my skin, and yet I have never felt that way. It is not the way they look at me as the way I look at them. I'm fine the way I am." He is very fine indeed.

The colour question does not only arise between black and white, but between black and black too. At times it can become more delicate for its own closeness. Just an example from a well-known personality:

> "Joyce was a good-looking woman in the university. One day I asked her if she was going to the Black Students' Association meeting. She looked at me funny, then started shaking her head like a baby who doesn't want what it sees on the spoon. 'I'm not black'. Joyce said, 'I'm *multiracial*.' Then she started telling me about her father, who *happened* to be Italian and was the sweetest man in the world; and her mother, who *happened* to be part African and part French and part Native American and part something else. 'Why should I have to choose between them?' she asked me. Her voice cracked, and I thought she was going to cry. 'It's not white people who are making me choose. Maybe it used to be that way, but now they're willing to treat me like a person. No – it's *black people* who always have to make everything racial. *They're* the ones making me choose. *They're* the ones who are telling me that

I can't be who I am'." (Barack Obama, Dreams from My Father, Three Rivers Press, New York 2004)

One more testimony to lighten up the racial tension with a bit of humour from someone who had to fight in the street and at school and with herself to find her place in society, in the University, in television. She knows how to make us smile.

"Are you black or white?" Michael, a popular fourth-grade boy, asked me. We were around the corner from my house preparing to pick teams for a kickball game.

I knew I should have played with the black kids today, I thought as I glanced longingly down the street at the three black girls jumping rope. I wondered if it would be too obvious if I dashed away from the white kids and hopped into their rope.

It seemed the kickball game was on hold until I answered Michael, so I gave the response I'd been trained to give, the sentence that was as much a part of my childhood as knowing my phone number and the proper way to sit when wearing a skirt.

"My mom is black and my dad is white", I said.

"So you're a zebra!" Michael said. The kickball group gasped and giggled in amazement, like Michael was a comedic genius for calling someone who's mixed with black and white a zebra. If he were truly witty, he would have called me a panda or a penguin, I thought.

"Zebra!" another boy shouted, and the virus spread, infecting two more boys until there was only one boy not chanting the word. Michelle and Heather, two girls from my class, were laughing at the chant. The five boys, pleased with that bit of attention, decided that playing ring-around-the-zebra was more fun than kickball. "I am *not* a Zebra!" I yelled as they circled around me. Unfortunately, no one could hear my great comeback over five male voices, so I expressed my anger by violently kicking their ball toward the sewer and then turned the other way and sprinted home.

Once inside the door, I tried to tell my parents what had happened but only one sound dropped out of my mouth. "Zee-zee-zee-zee", I said to my parents, trying to hold back my tears and talk at the same time. My mother shot my father a look, snatched me by one arm, and smashed my face into her overly powdered chest. I wheezed and cried while my father paced back and forth.

Once the last tear had flowed from my eye to her Jean Naté-flavoured cleavage, my mother and dad went into the kitchen for a Grown Folks Meeting as in times of crisis. My father shouted,
"I'm going to kill those little sons of bitches."
"And you'll go to jail!"
"*They* should be in jail!"
My father came out of the kitchen with my mother trailing him.
"Jack, where are you going?" she asked.

"To tell their parents. I won't hit anybody", my father said, grabbing my hand. "Show me where they live."

"I don't know where they live", I said, still swiping teardrops from my cheeks.

"We'll go to every door until we find them", my father assured me.

Suddenly, every tear was worth it. We were going door-to-door to kick some racist ass. "Wait!" my mother yelled as we pushed through the screen door. I was afraid she was going to stop our mission, but she wanted only to wipe some of her bosom's baby powder off my nose. (That's my mother – how will you get people to stop teasing your daughter if you send her outside looking a mess?) Once she had wiped my face with a dab of saliva, it was time to go racist-boy-hunting.

My father saw Michelle and asked her where the boys lived. After we rang the bell, a man and woman cautiously answered the door.

"Can I help you?" the man asked.

"Yes, you can", my father said. Your son Jimmy called my daughter a zebra."

"Oh, God", Jimmy's mother said. She turned and shouted, "Jimmeee!" Jimmy came running down the stairs, stopping short of the last step when he saw me and my father.

"Did you call this girl a zebra?" Jimmy's fatl_er asked.

"Yeah, but I wasn't the only one."

"I don't care who else did it. You apologize to her!" his father screamed, veins bulging from his neck.

"I'm sorry", Jimmy said, more to the carpet than to me.

"Are you okay with that?" my father asked me.

Are you okay with that? is one of those questions you shouldn't ask kids. Kids don't understand that some questions aren't meant to be answered truthfu¹iy. I did not know I was supposed to say, *Yes, I'm okay with that.*

"No", I said, turning to Jimmy's father. "Is he going to get a beating?" I asked.

"Angela", my father said, but by then the mother had said, "Yes, he is most certainly getting a beating. Jimmy started crying and flew back up the stairs. My father and I came back home in triumph. (Angela Nissel, Mixed, Villard, New York, 2006, p. 26)

A teaser. Where would you choose to be born in your next life? With which colour on your skin? In any case, remember: whatever you are *is* beautiful.

AN INDIAN WORD

The word "non-violence" was given to the world by India. It is negative in its form *a-himsa*, but this is precisely because the positive concept underlying it is so vast, so wide, so deep that it is best defined by negating its opposite and leaving open the term to all the fullness and the richness of an idea and an ideal that is a summary of morality and a way of life all by itself. Sanskrit, as other languages do, often uses to its advantage the grammatical twist of the negative particle *"a"* to express totality by negating partiality, which makes the expression "non-violence" into a wholly open and universal positive term. The word *Ahimsa* has entered the world vocabulary, and has brought with it a blessing and a hope to humankind in a dark moment of its history.

India was the first country in world history to obtain freedom from a colonial power, and a power like the British Empire at that, without fighting a war of independence. The Jewel of the Crown left the crown without a field battle or a violent wrenching. This is both a historical and a historic fact of the greatest significance, a planetary achievement, a decisive turning point in the flood of strife, violence and blood that has engulfed humankind for centuries. History textbooks are full of the independence wars every colony fought against its corresponding colonial power, and the whole American continent from north to south fought mortal battles in a long list of uprisings and campaigns and victories and defeats in dates schoolchildren have to memorise even today for their exams. India's example changed all that, created a momentous precedent, and paved the way for the peaceful transition of power in many territories of Asia and Africa. This should never be forgotten.

It is true that not every Indian is a Mahatma, and we cannot boast of pristine innocence when there are clashes in our own land and blood over our frontiers, but the moral values of *ahimsa* and *shanti* (peace) are enshrined in the Indian heart, and it is by sharing them with a world that needs them today more than ever that we can ourselves strengthen them within us and build around them our own specific and valuable identity. An American friend tells me: "There is an Indian in my office. When things at times get hot and tempers fly, I look at the Indian. He is always peaceful, self-composed and unruffled. Just looking at him I calm down and can rejoin the discussion in peace." *Ahimsa* and *shanti* go indefectibly together. We must calm down in our daily life if we want to remain peaceful and non-violent under pressure.

Here is an Indian's perception of the same reality in a charming first person narrative of a daily life episode:

"I learned a lesson in the importance of slowing down during my first Christmas in Berkeley. It was 1960, and I was still new to American ways. I went down to the post office to send a package to my mother in India. As I neared the sedate old building at the corner of Allston Way and Milvia, erected in a period when the pace of life was slower, I noticed cars double-parked and people darting up and down the broad granite steps. Inside was a scene of frustration, exasperation, and sometimes outright anger.

Crowd or no crowd, I needed to mail my package. I joined a long queue and stood patiently watching the scene around me. I enjoy watching life's passing show, and I have found that there is no need to look for extraordinary situations to find insight and inspiration.

On this occasion, everyone was giving unintended lessons in how to put yourself under pressure. A detached observer would have found the scene amusing. One fellow in front of me was bouncing up and down as if he were on a pogo stick. He was in such a hurry that he just had to release his nervous energy somehow, and with people pressing you in front and behind, the only direction possible is up.

Then I felt a hot breath on the back of my collar. The gentleman at the back of me was also in a hurry, and *he* was expending his nervous energy by blowing hot air down my neck. 'Well', I thought, 'Christmas is the time for expressions of good will.' So I just turned around. 'Please take my place', I told him. 'I'm not in a hurry.' He was so distracted that he didn't hear me. He just said brusquely, 'What?' - 'Take my place', I repeated. 'I have time. I'm in no hurry at all.' He stared, and then he began to relax. I felt the atmosphere around us begin to change. He apologised for being in such a hurry and mumbled something about being double-parked.

Slowly the queue moved forward. The young woman at the counter was probably a college student filling in for the holidays, and she was making mistake after mistake – giving the wrong stamps, giving wrong change – while people complained and corrected her. I could see that she was getting more and more upset; and the more upset she got, the more mistakes she made and the longer each transaction took. All because everybody was in a hurry! If the scene had ever had any Christmas cheer, it was evaporating rapidly.

I'm fond of students; I was a professor for many years. So when it came to my turn at the window, I said, 'I'm from India. Take your time.' She looked as if she couldn't believe it. But she smiled and relaxed, and she gave me the right change and the right stamps too. I thanked her and wished her a merry Christmas.

As I walked out, I noticed that the man behind me returned her smile. The whole room had relaxed a little; there was even a ripple of laughter at the end of the queue. Pressure is contagious, but so is good will. Just one person slowing down, one person not putting others under pressure, helps everyone else to relax too." (Eknath Easwaran, Take Your Time, p. 11)

The author rightly relates this attitude to Gandhi:

"I had the living example of Gandhi. Very, very few people in human history have accomplished more than Gandhi. Not many people even have the colossal vitality he had. But he generally looked so relaxed that a superficial observer might have thought he was lazy. If you look at some of the pictures of Gandhi, he looks so relaxed that he reminds me of our cat. Our cat just sits quietly at the foot of a tree, so restful that you think she is sleeping. Then, without any warning, you see a blur of half a dozen cats in the air. Such an explosion of movement! I always wonder where all this energy comes from. To look at her, she seems absolutely static; but when in action, she becomes not just one cat but half a dozen.

Gandhi was like that. When you looked at him, he looked so quiet, so gentle, so mild, that it took a long time for the British to understand that just as a cat becomes half a dozen cats in the air, Gandhi became four hundred million human beings when he stirred the unconscious aspirations of the Indian people."
(Ib p. 29)

Gandhi brought to bear on the national problems the attitude he had learned from his Jain ayah in his childhood and had imbibed from readings and sermons and family and tradition in his education. He coined the words, "civil disobedience", "peaceful resistance", "holding on to truth", and trained the nation in their spirit and their practice. He was a teacher to the whole nation and, through it, to the world. The lesson he taught, though deeply embedded in the mentality and tradition of the people of India, was an entirely new one on political battlefields, and his classroom was the whole country of millions in its massive uprising, which made the learning difficult at the beginning. He launched the peaceful independence movement and spelled out its conditions. People followed him, but popular feelings run high, and in an early incident a mob set fire to a police station at Chauri Chaura near Gorakhpur in North India, in which as many as 22 policemen were killed. Gandhi immediately called off the whole movement. Independence was not to be bought with blood. India came to a standstill. Other political leaders failed to understand Gandhi and urged that the movement should go on, even if marred by a few unavoidable incidents like that, as it would be very difficult to set it in motion again if it was just suppressed. But Gandhi stood firm. No freedom with violence. Rabindranath

Tagore, in deep unity with the Mahatma and with the people, uttered his sombre appraisal of the situation: "A dark cloud has descended on India. We know we have the final goal in our destiny, but we do not have the way." Then Gandhi found the way. He announced to the Viceroy of India and to the world at large that he would proceed on foot from his Sabarmati Ashram in Ahmedabad to Dandi on the coast where he would collect a handful of salt at the seashore in defiance of the salt laws that had nationalised the industry and forbad any such action by individuals.

Salt was a meaningful symbol, and Gandhi knew the value of symbols – at a time well before the culture of the image. In India salt is called *sab-ras,* meaning "all-taste", as it seasons food and renders it pleasant to the palate; it is also important in the tropics where heat brings it out in white, granular, salty perspiration on the forehead and it has to be replaced abundantly for the health of the organism; and then salt in the Orient is also a symbol of hospitality and loyalty. If you have "eaten my salt", that is, if you have been my guest and I your host and you have eaten in my home, you and I are for ever bound with a bond of friendship and fidelity that unites us through any length of time and any differences in race or religion or status. Another word for "salt" is *nimak,* and the word *nimakhalal* means "true to salt", that is "loyal", while *nimakharam* is "false to salt", that is "traitor". Salt was and is important in India for its substance and for its meaning. And then it had become at the time an instrument and a symbol of England's domination over India, as Indians could not, under strict laws, collect by themselves a product they so much appreciated and needed and could be just collected near the sea. So Gandhi defied the laws. He did it in his own inimitable way, informing the authorities, announcing his itinerary, choosing 78 companions, and walking in 23 days the 385 kilometres to the coast where he bent down, scooped with his hand a lump of salty mud, heated it in a burner and obtained a handful of salt in open and public defiance of the law.

The whole world had held its breath as the Mahatma advanced day by day in his purposeful march against the British Empire. A peaceful army out to conquest unarmed the vast land before them. There was no television in those days, but press and radio followed every step of the unique procession to its climax at the seashore and reported to an expectant world the scenario, the speeches, the meaning and the scenes of the worldwide drama. Gandhi was put to jail. Peaceful volunteers, abreast elbow to elbow in columns of six, advanced with steady, measured steps towards the iron gates of the Dharasana Salt Works to manifest their protest with their presence. A British sergeant stood in front of the gates, wielded an iron-pointed stick, and hit with it those that approached the gate till they fell down or retreated or were taken back by attending nurses. A Sikh volunteer with his white turban on his head came right in front of the British sergeant. The sergeant hit him brutally with his stick over his head. The Sikh volunteer fell down, peace volunteers approached and took him away in a stretcher as his head was bleeding under his white turban and he was unconscious. He slowly regained consciousness, stanched his blood, adjusted his stained turban and joined again the slowly advancing column of volunteers to the gates. He advanced, approached, and stood again in front of the same British sergeant with his iron-pointed stick. The sergeant hardened his face, lifted his stick, measured the blow, hesitated for a moment, then slowly he brought his stick down, pressed it under his left arm, lifted his right hand, brought it to his forehead in a military salute, clicked his heals, turned round, and walked away.

An American radio correspondent had followed the scene on location and had described it on the spot blow by blow in a live commentary that went round the world and gave sound and profile to the new concept of non-violence. The British sergeant saluting the non-violent volunteer. Everything was there. The world knew it. India was free.

LESSON NUMBER FOUR

Once I was in a Hindu home sitting on the floor in a corner and carrying on my writing work there while two children, obviously schoolmates, were doing their homework together by my side. One of them looked at the day's task and this brief dialogue reached my ears:

- What do we have to write our essay today about?
- About someone in history.
- Who was that?
- Wait a minute.
- Well, tell me.
- Yes, Mahatma Gandhi.
- And who was Gandhi?
- Lesson number four.

That was that. Lesson number four. The Father of the Nation, the Champion of Independence, the Mahatma, was only Lesson Number Four. A lesson in the textbook, a page in history, an old memory. For their parents Gandhiji had been a living experience, they knew his voice and revered his picture, they quoted his name and strove to live up to his principles; but for their children Gandhi was just Lesson Number Four. When the film "Gandhi", loaded with Oscars, was shown in India, everybody liked it, but then most people were surprised by it. They didn't know the story. And Gandhi's story is well worth knowing and sharing with the world.

He taught with his life, or, as he liked to say, "my life is my message", and his witty and timely anecdotes were the open textbook of the new science of political freedom. To give a national dimension to his teaching, one of the first things Gandhi did was the founding of the Navjivan Press in Ahmedabad to print his word and spread his message to the four corners of the subcontinent. People took on from there and passed on eagerly the teaching from mouth to mouth as the best means of communication media ever. Every gesture was a lesson, every episode a lecture on the art of independence, of character building, of readiness to self rule.

Gandhi was in jail at Yeravda as a political prisoner. An old inmate of the Jail, a Somali black called Adam, was appointed as his warder to keep watch over him with the idea that, being a stranger, he would not let himself be influenced by Gandhi. Still, the good man took quite a liking to him, sensed his greatness, and served him with reverence. After a few days he came stealthily to Gandhi and showed him a copy of *The Times of India* while he smiled since he knew all the other political prisoners were always eager to get the newspaper which he some days managed to smuggle for them, and he said: "It is today's paper. You'll enjoy it." Gandhi refused to touch the paper, and, to the poor man's discomfiture, he even scolded him: "You know as well as I do that we are not allowed to read newspapers in jail. It is the rule, and I obey the rules. Take it back at once and never come with that to me again." Gandhi wanted his people to obey rules, and so he began by obeying them himself – even in jail. He was forming a nation of obedient, disciplined, law-abiding citizens, and he projected through his behaviour the image he wanted to be imprinted in every heart. The anecdote would be broadcast at once through the grapevine, and people would learn. This episode has a happy ending, though. Adam resorted to a trick, and pleaded with Gandhi: "All right. You are a great man and you do not want to read the paper. I understand. But please, do it for me. Y come from a far-off land in Africa and have no news of it and I cannot read the paper. Please, read it for me so that I can get some news from my country." Gandhi smiled, understood the trick, took the paper, there were in it news of war in Somaliland and he read them out to Adam. Adam went out smiling like a child and saying, "Gandhi read the paper, Gandhi read the paper! I got him to read the paper!" Gandhi knew how to keep the rules, and how to make people happy.

Gandhi's wife, Kasturba, was one day allowed to visit him in jail. The visit was to last for half an hour in the presence of the jail superintendent. He, again, like the man of the newspaper, was full of respect and reverence for the exceptional prisoner, and treated him with delicate deference. Gandhi and Kasturba sat themselves at the two ends of a small table and exchanged their first greetings while the superintendent, as unobtrusively as possible, paced up and down the room in the background. Soon he quietly left the room so that the saintly couple could talk freely by themselves. After half an hour he came back and told Gandhi with a pleased smile:

- I hope you had a good talk together.
- Talk? No. We didn't speak.
- What do you mean? You didn't talk all this while?
- That's right, we didn't talk after you left. You see, I know the jail rules, and the conversation with visitors has to take place in the presence of the superintendent. While you were here we did talk a little as you saw,

but once you left, as I suppose you did to attend to some urgent business, I knew we couldn't talk and so we just kept quiet until you returned. The half hour has now passed and the visit is over.

Gandhi would not let an occasion pass to teach the nation, even at the price of not being able to speak with his wife. Small things and passing incidents were the parables that brought the teaching to the crowds, and Gandhi's life was an open university for all the world to graduate in.

Here is one more example of his way of dealing with the smallest as a projection to the greatest. A true example of non-violence, this time in the personal friction of family life. The narrative is Kakasaheb Kalelkar's:

"A young man of a family related to Gandhi had been engaged to marry a girl. The engagement is taken very seriously in Hindu society, and the girl's parents were already preparing the wedding. But then the young man rebelled and refused to marry the girl. This was a calamity. They all tried to persuade him, but without success. Finally the bride's family, whose honour was particularly at stake as it would be difficult to find another partner for the girl after that awkward situation, came to Gandhi. He was their kinsman and was the leader of the nation, and with his authority and his great powers of persuasion he would certainly be able to teach the rebel his duty and make him agree to the wedding. They did feel bad to have to take the time of the Father of the Nation for such a private matter, but they were helpless. Gandhi agreed. He spoke with the young man, sometimes alone, sometimes before all the relatives, with all patience several times a day for three days. All could see how worthless and ill-mannered the young man was.

Finally the young man accepted. Before Gandhi and the whole family gathered together he formally declared that he was ready to marry the girl. The girl's relatives breathed relief and thanked Gandhi profusely. But then Gandhi became serious and asked the boy to leave the room. He then told the family: 'You have his consent. You can go and settle the wedding tomorrow. But you have seen for three days what the mind of the boy is, and you are witnesses of the difficulty with which I could bring him round. Do you still want this man to marry your daughter?'

The eldest man in the family, on whom the final decision depended, froze. I kept looking at him and could see the storm that was raging in his mind. For a long time his lips could not shape any word. Neither a Yes nor a No could pass through them. All the time Gandhi just kept looking at him with his piercing sight. Finally the man melted and said: 'Dear Mahatma, you are right. Let the boy be free.' Gandhi called the boy and told him he was released from the bond.

They all left, and Gandhi returned to his work. But I could see that a gentle smile played on his lips the whole day." (Kaka Kalelkar, *Bapuni Jhankhi* p. 74)

Gandhi could have told his relatives from the start to leave the boy alone, as he knew he would be doing at the end. But he went through the whole process of getting first the boy to agree and then setting him free, thus gaining credibility, understanding and agreement, and setting down an object lesson of family dealings and government management. He was a true leader.

ZEN AND YOGA

"Zen" is another word given by India to the world, this time in a roundabout way, a little in disguise. It is the Japanese pronunciation of the Chinese character for the Sanskrit word *"dhyan"* which migrated from India to China with the first Buddhism. It is a great word. It means attention, contemplation, concentration, meditation. The word is used today in daily life in North Indian languages. Its use ranges from the blaring loudspeaker at the airport, "Your attention, please!" ("attention" is *dhyan*) to the Buddha in full lotus posture, index and thumb together, eyes closed and serene countenance in profound meditation ("meditation" is *dhyan*). It is again an Oriental characteristic as against the hurry, the rush, the short-sightedness, the superficiality of much of Western activities and attitudes.

By the way, Buddha also came from India, only that he has become so universal that people often forget his origin. His temples are not only in India, where the Ajanta and Ellora caves exhibit in the gentle curve of the ancient rock some of the most artistic, devout, inspiring, eternal stone statues of the prince who became an ascetic, but also throughout the Far East from Myanmar to Japan and from monasteries to markets. Orange robed monks bow before the Lying Buddha of Chaukhtatgyi while young

Chinese communists in their jeans wear jade images of the Buddha round their necks in Tiananmen Square. *Buddham sharanam gacchami.* (I seek refuge in the Buddha.)

Dhyan is both a religious exercise and a practical attitude. We need concentration in all that we do and in all that we live, and the union of our mental attitude during the day with our pointed meditation at its set times is the secret of intimate peace of soul on one hand and effective work and professional excellence on the other. The following story is told in many versions by many masters, and embodies in itself the core of Indian spirituality and practicality.

A disciple went to a master to ask for training in the ways of the spirit and of life. The master gave him a vessel full of oil to the brim and told him to go around the city without spilling a drop of oil. The disciple took carefully the vessel in both his hands, started on his way, kept steadily his eyes on it, minded each step with full attention, followed ways and streets and squares and lanes, and returned to the *ashram* (another untranslatable word!) or school of his master with the vessel intact. The master told him:

- Fine. You've gone round the city and you haven't spilled a drop of oil. Tell me now, what did you see in the city? Give me a description of streets and squares and buildings and palaces and the people and the animals. What did you see?
- I saw nothing, master. I was so concentrated on the oil to fulfil your order of not spilling it that I did not lift my eyes from the ground and the vessel and saw nothing.
- Very well, then. Now go again tomorrow in the same manner with the vessel and the oil and the care not to spill a drop, and then on your way back give me a

detailed description of the city, its buildings and its people.

The disciple did as bidden, started on his way, paid attention to everything around, came back, and gave his master a detailed account of what he had seen and had heard and had noticed all along his way. The master listened to him attentively and told him:
- Very well. You noticed everything around. Now, what about the oil?
- Oh, sorry, master! I hadn't noticed. I see now that the vessel is half empty. I forgot all about the oil. It must have spilled over without my realising it.
- Very well, then. Now you have your task. Do this every day, though changing your path daily for new sensations; pay attention both to the city life and to the oil, and the day you come back telling all you have seen without having spilt a drop of oil, your training will be over.

This parable is a popular illustration of the Buddha's own teaching. When he was asked what monks should do in order to attain perfection, he answered:

"When the monk walks, he is fully in his walking, when he stands he is fully in his standing, when he sits down he is fully in his sitting down, and when he lies down he is fully in his lying down. When he looks he is fully intent on looking, when he stretches out his hand he is intent on stretching out his hand, when he dresses he is intent on dressing, and, in the same way, when he eats, drinks, chews, or tastes, or performs any other action, he commits himself fully to what he is doing with perfect understanding of his action."

Walk when you walk, eat when you eat. It would seem that we all do that. In fact, we seldom do it. We are experts at doing what we are not doing and being where we are not. Dialogue between disciple and master:

- Master, when can I go home?
- Son, where are you now?

We should always and everywhere be at home. And home is wherever we are at the moment. Be in touch. Be aware. Do what you do and be where you are. To do two things at a time means giving only half attention to each. Reading Gandhi's correspondence I found an instructive example on this point. Gandhi had popularised the use of the spinning wheel as a symbol and a means of self-sufficiency and of national independence, he sat at it for a length of time every day and expected his followers to do the same. They did. His secretary, Mahadev Desai, while in jail as a political prisoner, took advantage of the situation and spent the greatest part of the day at the spinning wheel. Another political prisoner in the same prison was Abba Saheb, who knew French, and offered to teach Mahadev Desai French which would be useful for Gandhi's international correspondence. Mahadev put the two things together, started learning French while spinning, and proudly wrote to Gandhi to tell him of his progress. He had not expected the kind of answer he got. Here is Gandhi's letter:

"I am distressed at the news about yourself. How can you, who are so close to me, have misunderstood me so badly? Whatever we do requires our full attention, and do not think that because spinning is a material occupation it can be done mechanically and without care. Whatever we do has to be done well, with all our mind and all our heart. One thing at a time, and every work done to perfection. Study French by all means, but stop the spinning wheel while you learn French. Do you not remember having discussed with me what

Romain Rolland says in his book on Beethoven about his concentration while playing the piano? And is the spinning wheel any less important than the piano? I feel pained to see that you have not yet realised the holiness of the spinning wheel, as indeed of everything we do."

I have a personal footnote to this episode. Narayan Desai, son of Mahadev Desai, who strove to keep up the Gandhian spirit after the independence of India, invited me once to give a talk to his Moral Rearmament volunteers in Vedchhi, South Gujarat, and I accepted. We both stood alone on a large stage in the open air before the eager crowd. He introduced me most graciously, motioned me to the mike, sat on the floor at my feet where a spinning wheel was brought to him, and went on spinning by my side during my full lecture. At the end, he stood up and presented me publicly with the spool of cotton yarn he had spun during my lecture. At least something useful to show for the time of my lecture. But not a compliment to my lecture in Gandhi's view. I didn't tell the son about Gandhi's letter to his father.

Dhyan (or Zen) is part of Yoga, (more exactly, the seventh stage of the eightfold path of Yoga, just before the final *Samadhi* – another great word), and Yoga is also a gift of India to the world. The word is now part of the universal vocabulary worldwide, and its meaning is significant. "Yoga" in Sanskrit means "union". The word is not foreign to European languages, as from the Sanskrit *"yoga"* comes the Greek *"dsugon"*, the Latin *"yugum"*, the Spanish *"yugo"*, the English *"yoke"*, which all mean the same in different languages: the long piece of wood that unites the necks of two oxen for their labour on the field. All is yoga, or union. All that unites, reconciles, fits, meets, becomes one after being many and united after being dispersed is Yoga. We, in our shaky instability, are scattered, dissipated, distracted, divided, and to become firmly united within ourselves, to become whole, to become one again, we need the attention to reality, to facts, to sensations rather than imagination, to the present moment rather than to past or future, to the here-and-now rather than to the there-and-then. We need attention, we need concentration, we need yoga. In the unity of being is the strength of its existence.

Ahimsa, Yoga, Dhyan (Zen). Words are humankind's abiding treasure. India has given three treasures to the world.

A IS A

This is now more than words. The point I'm going to touch upon here means more to me than most of the others I'm making in these pages, while probably it will mean next to nothing to most readers. For me it is essential. My Aristotelian background – no boast – is responsible for the shock that unexpectedly awaited me in the East that is East while the West always was and is and will continue to be impenitently West, and of the transformation it brought to my way of thinking, understanding, and living. The event literally changed my mind.

As a westerner, my mental setup came from Aristotle via Thomas Aquinas, Descartes, Newton and Kant. Hegel, influenced precisely by eastern thought, did try to reject Aristotle but with little popular success. We all in the West are children of Aristotle, whether we know it or not. Our way of thinking, our principles, our logic come simply from his "Metaphysics" in both letter and spirit. Even if we have not framed a single syllogism in our lives, our mind knows its rules, and it is evident to high heaven that "All men are mortal; but Socrates is a man; therefore Socrates is mortal". And that is that.

The three principles that form the basis of Aristotelian thinking are well-known:

Principle of Identity: Being is Being.
Principle of Contradiction: Being is not Non-Being.
Principle of Excluded Middle: Whatever is, is Being or Non-being.

If this sounds too poetical, we can express the three principles mathematically as,

A is A
A is not non-A
Whatever is, is A or non-A

Thursday is Thursday. Thursday is not Non-Thursday. Whatever day of the week it is, it is Thursday or Non-Thursday. Plain enough. That's the way our mind works from home dialogues to lawyers' arguments. Everything else comes from that. It is actually a deep intellectual joy, a mental treat, an academic wonder to see how from these three principles the whole towering edifice of western thought is built up brick by brick in strict cohesion, firmness and beauty. That was how I felt, how I thought, how I lived. Being *is* Being.

Once in India, I learned languages, read ancient and recent literature, delved into the Mahabharata, studied the Bhagavad Gita. And there, in the planes of Kurukshetra, on the eve of the epic encounter between Kauravas and Pandavas, in the awesome solitude of the war chariot whose charioteer was Shri Krishna himself and whose valiant warrior was Arjuna, I listened to the words that explained in rhythmical verses the battle that life is and the metaphysical riddle that human existence has always been in the cosmic accents and the revealing insights of The Lord's Canticle (Bhagavad Gita). It was there I read in wonder:

"The Lord of Lords spoke:
'Oh Arjuna,
As the sun I give heat and shadow,

I withhold and I send forth rain;
I am both immortality and death,
Being and Non-Being I am!'"
(9:19)

Being and Non-Being. *"Sat"* and *"A-sat".* The essence
of reality *(sat)* and the essence of nothingness *(asat).* The
fullness of truth (again *sat),* and the emptiness of falsehood
(a-sat also, with the negative *'a').* Everything and nothing.
Yes and No. A and non-A. I am that. So simply and clearly
and definitively and constructively said. In the battlefield
of life between fighting armies and dying warriors. Being
and Non-Being. Both are the same. With Arjuna faithfully
listening. That was a radical shock to all my mental and
logical setup. Goodbye to Aristotle!

My first realisation when I recovered from the blow
was an utter wonderment at how a whole country, a
whole civilisation, a long and noble history and millions
of people through it, my actual friends and neighbours in
India could live happily and merrily without the Principle
of Contradiction! So, it was not all that necessary after all! I
smiled and went out to walk the streets, just to look at people
around me who came and went, walked and talked, smiled
and laughed while they – oh wonder of wonders! – did not
believe in the Principle of Contradiction and nobody seemed
to miss it. I felt like approaching unconcerned walkers,
stop them, bow to them and then ask them how they felt
about the Principle of Contradiction, how they reconciled
themselves to the fact that A could be Non-A, Being could
be Non-Being, how they managed to live without Aristotle.
Then I imagined I would touch their feet and ask their
blessing in awe and reverence while we together repeated
the verse of the Gita. "Being and Non-Being I am." This was
truly another world. I had touched rock bottom and I knew
it. Everything else, every other difference between East and

West, every nuance and every clash followed from that; every attitude, every belief, every argument was marked by this essential, inborn, eternal divergence. There truly was a chasm between East and West, and it went right down to the very foundations of human thought. Though it didn't even show on the surface. For the West, Being is never Non-Being. For the East, it always is. Now I knew it. Being and Non-Being I am.

Bertrand Russell mentioned once in an informal conversation that if a system admits of a single contradiction, it admits all. A friend challenged him: "Then prove that if zero is equal to one, you are the pope." Russell argued at once: "$0 = 1$. Add 1 to each side. $1 = 2$. Now reverse: $2 = 1$. The pope and I are two, but two is equal to one, so there is only one person and I am the pope." Anything follows.

Shock followed shock. My own mathematical training gave later a jolt to the Principle of Excluded Middle also when, together with the traditional day-to-day binary logic of yes and no, it accepted matter-of-factly ternary and even multi-valued logics where the alternatives were widened and the world of thought was not any more black and white. About that time, too, I came across this text of one of the great six masters of early Buddhism, Sanjayin Vairattiputra, who answered thus king Ajatshatru's question whether there was an afterlife:

"I cannot say that there is;
I cannot say that there is not;
I cannot say that there is and there is not at the same time;
I cannot say that there is not and there is no 'is not' at the same time." (*Nirvana Sutra*, 115)

Crystal clear. Though we don't know the look on king Ajatshatru's face while he listened to his court chaplain deliver his answer. In any case, Aristotle was out of this one too. And here is, to lighten up the metaphysics, an example to show that such tongue-twisters can have even practical value. Very practical indeed in the East.

> The Mulla Naseruddin was one day approached by the owner of a field who showed him the documents that proved the field belonged to him. The Mulla examined them and decreed: "You are fully right."

> Later, another claimant to the same field came and showed Naseruddin the proofs that the field belonged to him. He saw them and answered him: "You are fully right."

> Naseruddin's wife had been present on both occasions, and when all had left, she told her husband: "You tell one man that the field belongs to him, and then you tell his opponent that the field belongs to him. This is absurd!" The Mulla answered: "You are fully right."

Ternary logic of a kind. In fact, modern mathematics and modern physics were by then performing experiments and using language that approached more Vairattiputra's vagueness than Aristotle's dichotomy. Though scientific findings did not influence practical minds any more than Einstein's relativity affects the railway timetable.

There remained, though, Aristotle's foundation stone still in its place: A is A. Principle of Identity. That seemed unchangeable and unchallengeable. Evident and clear. A had to be A in any case and above all things. Being is Being. Whatever was, had to be what it was and it could not be otherwise. But then, with time and patience, the day for the First Principle came too in my life. The great monument of the Mahayana Buddhism, the *Vajracchedika Prajnaparamita Sutra,* had the following gem:

"The *dharma* that is the *dharma,* is not anymore the *dharma.*" (6)

Dharma is another great Sanskrit word. It means nature, duty, essence, rule, justice, religion..., in a word, A. The word and its meaning is, by its nature, active, growing, living, and if it is imprisoned in the mould of straight formulae it ceases to be what it is, as the electron when stopped to measure its mass and its speed is not anymore what it was in mass and speed. The A that is A, is not anymore A. Life is not static. Truth is not stone. Being is not just Being. This did away with the first principle, the Principle of Identity. Total liberation.

Eastern thought works more through stories and parables than through equations and definitions. We can sense all the rational weight of all these abstract considerations with a chuckle and a smile in a simple and enlightening wisdom story. This is a favourite one on the same point of interior liberation:

The master sends his disciple on a long pilgrimage to Buddhist shrines in distant lands. When the disciple comes back, the master welcomes him back and asks him:

- How was your pilgrimage, son?
- It was a wonderful experience, master.
- What makes you say that, my child?
- I have seen the largest statue of the Buddha in the world!
- You must be very strong then, my son.
- Why do you say that, my master?
- Because I see you are still carrying it on your shoulders.

Wisdom lesson of the East to the West.

THE PEACOCK AND THE COBRA

The word *dharma,* just mentioned, deserves attention. It is the first of the "Four Achievements" *(Char Purushartha)* with which Hinduism describes the aim and direction of human life. As the meaning of life is the basic questions for all humans, from which our attitude to things and our whole existence depends, and as the question has been proposed, discussed, meditated and abandoned in turn by all races and civilisations in all countries and ages, it will be enlightening to see how traditional Indian mentality sees it. The Four Achievements are *Dharma* (see meanings above), *Artha* (wealth), *Kama* (pleasure), *Moksha* (liberation). Quite a programme for life indeed!

It is a pity *dharma* has been inconsiderately, superficially and universally translated as "religion". Here is a teaser: "The *dharma* of the cow is to give milk." This sentence makes perfect sense in any Indian language, and no sense at all in English where the literal translation "the religion of the cow is to give milk" just makes us smile. A very pious cow indeed. Dictionaries mislead. My *dharma,* in its true meaning, is pre-eminently my own self, my totality as a person, my most me in me. So the point of The First Achievement is that I have to be myself, to bring out my own nature, to fulfil my duty, to achieve fullness in life. This is the first aim that precedes and summarises all the four.

The second is "wealth". Material wellbeing, which is what *artha* means, is by no means ignored in the Hindu view of life. It is part of the human existence, both as a means to a satisfying life and as a feedback for one's performance in society. Doing well in life is regarded in the Orient as a sign of being good at heart, as the material expression of the person's spiritual advancement. Poverty is a punishment for past misdeeds, and wealth is a recompense for virtue. One of the classic books of ancient India is the *Arthashastra* (literally "Treatise of Wealth", while the term *arthashastra* is now simply and rightly the modern term for "economics") written in the fourth century B.C. by "the world's first management guru", Kautilya, for the king Chandragupta Maurya, grandfather of Ashoka the Great. His approach is so considerate that he has a full chapter on "Control over the senses", as, according to him, anger, lust, greed and pride would harm first the person and then society. Material goods help life, and the pursuing of economic welfare is part of the human destiny on earth.

The surprising element in the four-fold formula is *kama,* which literally means "sex" as everybody knows from the *Kamasutra,* and comes here as representative of all that is enjoyment and pleasure in a full human life. This is significantly and refreshingly oriental. Eastern cultures through ages have shown a healthy, direct, matter-of-fact approach to sex, long removed from the obsession, the condemnation, the prudery, the trauma, the guilt complex that in the West have traditionally accompanied the very mention of sex..., till modern reaction has, of course, gone to the other extreme of total permissiveness. But the scars remain. In traditional India the body was not an enemy, and sex was not a taboo. Witness is the *Kamasutra,* just mentioned, which expounds sex with academic detachment, and the temples of Khajuraho which express the same teaching in stone. I'm going to give here a less known example, chosen from my mathematical background, apologising for having already used this illustration in another book of mine. It belongs here. I indulge in the luxury of quoting myself:

> "Bhaskaracharya is the name of the greatest mathematical genius in Indian history. His best-known work, the *Lilavati,* was written at the beginning of the twelfth century. The name of the book is touchingly poetical – as indeed is the whole book written in verse – as *lila* is the Sanskrit word for 'game', 'play', 'sport', and is even applied to the divine sport of creation on the playgrounds of nature. And Lilavati is the feminine proper noun for 'The Playful One', favourite name for a lovely child, a young girl, a beloved daughter. Such was Bhaskaracharya's only child, and the story of how her poetical name came to be on the title page of her father's abstract mathematical treatise is a treasured legend in Indian tradition.
>
> Lilavati's wedding was taking place, and the most important part of the ceremony was the fixing of the exact moment at which the 'joining of the hands' of bride and bridegroom by the officiating priest had to take place for an auspicious marriage. Her father himself had planned the calculation of that planetary instant in a way worthy of his mathematical knowledge and his poetical imagination. He bored an exact hole in a large lotus leaf on the surface of the waters in the pond of the garden at whose side they all sat for the ceremony, so calculated that water would flow gently in, and the moment the leaf sank would signal the astral conjunction that alone made the wedding possible. Exact mathematical calculation.

The ceremony began and the leaf was sinking on time, when the bride leaned over the water and a pearl from her necklace broke loose and slid unseen onto the chosen leaf. There it run to the centre of the leaf, stopped the essential hole, and the water stood still. Nobody noticed it. As time passed, however, people began to wonder, waited, looked carefully, and discovered the mishap. The unique instant at which the wedding could have taken place for a happy marriage had long past, and the bejewelled bride was condemned to unmarried existence.

It was then, to console his daughter in her grief, that her father did the only thing he could do. He told her: 'I will write a book that will last for ages, and I will put your name to it. You will become immortal.' How far the father's scholarship healed the daughter's sorrow we do not know, but the book is there with the name of the hapless girl on its cover: Lilavati.

Now, a mathematics book contains practical problems to be solved as exercises, and those examples are taken from daily occurrences, giving us a glimpse of the cultural life of the people in that time and country. The problems I solved at school were worded in terms of trains, rivers, towers, or football games. In my college studies at Madras University, they dealt with cricket games or business transactions. Today mathematical textbooks abound in problems about missiles and space vehicles and computers. What was, then, daily life and which were its common occurrences in the twelfth century in India? Here are some insights from the Lilavati, though we miss in translation the solemn beauty of its Sanskrit verses.

'A peacock is perched on a column nine cubits high. At the foot of the column is a cobra's hole. The peacock sees the snake at a distance three times the height of the column, crawling towards its hole, and dives to catch it. If the speed of the peacock is the same as the speed of the cobra, find at once, oh you worthy scholar, the distance from the base of the column to the point at which the peacock catches the snake.

[Answer: 12 cubits]

A king gives gifts to Brahmins for fifteen days. The first day he gives them four gold coins, the second nine, and so every day five more than the previous one. How many coins does he give on the whole?

[Answer: 585]

The god Shankar holds ten attributes in his ten hands: noose, goad, cobra, drum, skull, trident, sceptre, dagger, arrow, bow. If we combine all those attributes in all possible ways in his ten hands, how many different images of the god Shankar can we produce? And if you, oh worthy scholar, happen to be a devotee of god Vishnu, how many images of him can you depict with all the combinations of his four attributes, conch, wheel, mace, lotus?

[Answer: 3,628,800 for Shankar, and 24 for Vishnu. And now, watch for the next one:]

While a courtesan is making love to her lover, her pearl necklace snaps broken. One fifth of the pearls fall on the bed, one third on the floor, one sixth remain on her body, and one tenth in her lover's hands. If six pearls were left threaded in the necklace, can you say, O worthy worshipper of Shiva, how many pearls were there on the whole?'

Other examples follow on the number of arrows
Arjuna needed to subdue Karna in the Mahabharata
battle, on lakes and lotuses and clouds and swans.
And in the midst of them all, without provoking any
stir or causing an eyebrow to rise, blending with the
landscape and flowing with the current, stands the tale
of the courtesan and her lover. Sex must have been
quite a commonplace occurrence in those days when
it could be mentioned so matter-of-factly in a learned
treatise on mathematics.

I have written several mathematics textbooks for
school and college use in my life, and I can imagine
the hue and cry that would have been raised if I had
included in any of them a problem like the following:
'A prostitute is making love to a client. If the sum
of their ages is fifty, and the difference ten, and the
woman is younger than the man, find, oh you devoted
worshipper of the gods, their respective ages.' The
scandal would have reached the sky, the book would
have been banned, and I would have been declared
a corrupter of youth and made to drink the hemlock
like Socrates. I could have never got away with it.
Yet Bhaskaracharya did. I am in no way defending
prostitution, but I do find it irresistibly refreshing to
see sex mentioned nonchalantly together with lotuses
and peacocks and kings and gods by a senior scholar
and loving father in a learned treatise inscribed to his
virgin daughter. No titillation, no prudery, no Pharisaic
scandal, no Victorian taboo.

The answer to the problem is readily found. One-fifth
of the pearls plus one-third plus one-sixth plus one-
tenth plus six pearls equals the total number, which
we call x. That is:

$$x/5 + x/3 + x/6 + x/10 + 6 = x.$$

Clearing up the fractions and solving for the unknown, we find the number of pearls to be thirty.

Also, for those who may not know it, the peacock is the traditional enemy of the cobra." (Let Go of Fear, p.79)

The fourth and final element in the Indian definition of life's aims is the one we know least about. *Moksha* is liberation. Whatever we know about ourselves on this earth, we know that we are limited, incomplete, bounded. Removal of all bounds is liberation. We'll know more about it when we reach it. Meanwhile smile innocently with the wisdom of the East:

- Master, could you tell us what happens to us after death?
- I don't know.
- But you are a Zen master!
- Yes, but I am not a dead Zen master.

THE LOTUS OF A THOUSAND PETALS

Dharma, as we have seen, popularly means "religion". In the singular. The trouble comes when the singular becomes plural and religion becomes religions. The purest feeling in the human heart can become its darkest shadow, and people who are meant to be one in their Maker can kill one another in his name. Devout Hindus recite The Thousand Names of Vishnu while devout Muslims recite The Thousand Names of Allah. Thousand is human language for Infinite. Infinite is beyond us. God is above and beyond our concept of him, and by lovingly and feelingly giving him names we uncover the thousand facets of his being, and the more facets the diamond has, the more precious it becomes. One of the Sanskrit names for God is, again, The Lotus of a Thousand Petals. Each person, each faith, each creed adds its own contribution to the complete image (even atheists in their negation express something about The Inexpressible One), and it is the whole round crown of white beauty and soft touch that enhances the garden of our lives in the clear waters of mystic contemplation. The Lotus of a Thousand Petals. The fact that none of us can encompass the infinitude of God should draw us together to share experiences and compare concepts in gratitude to learn from one another and thus to grow in the knowledge of the One whose knowledge matters more to us than all other things, treasuring always our own tradition in full loyalty and fidelity, and ready to learn from those of others in openness and humility. This is ecumenism. And our age has the privilege and the responsibility to practice it in depth.

In Mumbai and many places around, there is a religious festival which puzzles those who for the first time watch it and see the crowds and witness the strange rite. It is *Ganesh Chaturthi* in honour of Shri Ganesh, the god with the elephant head, the son of Shiva and Parvati, the Remover of Obstacles, the one to be invoked at the beginning of each work, to have his image printed at the head of every wedding invitation, to be revered as the God of the Group which is what his name, Ganesh, means, *gan* being the word for "group" and *isha* meaning "god". On the fourth day of the bright fortnight of the month Bhadrapada clay images of Shri Ganesh, which have been worshipped the whole previous year and in a special manner for several days before the event, are brought in procession through the streets with canticles and flowers, are taken to the seashore along the golden curve of The Queen's Necklace, and are worshipped again on the sands of the beach. Then the devotees who have brought the images lift them up again, walk slowly into the waters with them on their heads, and gently lower the images into the sea to be swallowed, dissolved, dispersed by the incoming waves. What can the meaning of this strange rite be?

The rite has a deep theological meaning. However noble and artistic and meaningful and inspiring the images we shape of the divinity in our minds and in our temples may be, they are always limited by our own limited faculties, by our thought, our conception, our colours and our shapes. They represent a particular view but they do not exhaust the reality of the divinity. And so, while we venerate God as we imagine him, we are also ready to let go of that image, thus proclaiming that we have worshipped what we understood, we have acknowledged our limitation in understanding it, and we have professed our readiness to open ourselves to newer and deeper understandings of God as we persevere in our own faith and grow in our devotion. The old image was certainly a help to understand God, but as we advance in his love and knowledge it can become a hindrance by making God static, repeated, lifeless. Thus we first fashion the image – and then we reverently, lovingly, delicately let it down into the waters of his own creation in the sea. And this, which directly applies to the external image, applies equally to the mental image, to our verbal, conceptual, intellectual representations of God. We worship God as we know him, and then we open ourselves to know him in a deeper and newer way as he may show himself to us in our studies and in our prayers. As we grow in age, we correspondingly grow in our understanding of the world, of life, and of God. Dealing with him in prayer and worship through the years, we draw nearer to him and get to know him better. Our concept of God grows as our commitment to him grows. The secret to advance in the knowledge of God is to be ready to gently let down into the sea with all love and reverence the image we had venerated the previous year with equal love and reverence. This is the lesson of *Ganesh Chaturthi* as it is celebrated every year in Mumbai. Then the worshippers go back and fashion new images. The new image, of course, should now be at least a little different from last year's one. Only, maybe Mumbai artisans have not thought of that yet.

This festival, which existed from old, was popularised in Mumbai by Lokmanya Tilak, one of the first great figures of India's independence struggle. The British government, in its policy of preventing any popular movement in favour of independence, had outlawed all meetings and demonstrations in the streets of Mumbai. But Tilak found the way. He organised the popular processions in honour of Shri Ganesh. A religious procession, of course, was allowed, and the police, on government orders, cleared the streets and facilitated the moving of the crowds through the city to the sea. That was fine. What the British did not know was that Shri Ganesh was The Remover of Obstacles *(Vighnaharta)*, and the Obstacle to be removed was, of course... the British Government! Thus the procession was in fact a peaceful demonstration that united the people, kindled patriotism, showed strength, and made everybody happy through the streets of Mumbai under police protection. Politics, in this case, helped piety, and piety helped politics. *Ganpati Bappa Morya!* (The exclamation with which the image is thrown into the sea.)

Rabindranath Tagore has a beautiful parable to teach humility in our search for God and to remind us that all our knowledge of him is incomplete – and it had better stay that way. I read that page of his writings long ago and don't have it at hand, so the retelling will be in my own words, but the story is his.

A man in search of God wanted to find The House of God on earth, enter it, meet God, and thus bring to its final conclusion the task that had occupied him all his life: the search for God. He travelled through far-off lands, climbed mountains, waded rivers, crossed deserts, braved forests. He asked people, studied scriptures, consulted oracles, read the stars. Finally, after much struggle and long pilgrimages, he arrived in front of a majestic palace which bore above its main door the inscription: The House of God. He had found it! God was waiting for him behind that gate. One last step and the dream of his life would be his. The man climbed the long flight of white high marble steps to the gate, stood before the closed doors, and knocked thrice with his fist on the heavy door. He knocked again. He knocked a third time. Then a deep voice like thunder and storm was heard from inside: "Wait, I'm coming!"

The man heard the voice. He knew that was God, the God he had searched for all his life, the aim of all his wanderings, the fulfilment of his life. He was about to meet God himself and thus to end his quest. But then, when the door began to creak open, when the light filtered through the opening and a stately figure was sketched in the background, before he could see the face that appeared in it or meet the eyes that looked at him from it, he turned back, rushed down the long flight of white high marble steps and flew for his life without ever looking back.

He thought in his flight: If I see him now, what will the rest of my life be? Once the search is over, the aim of my life will also be over. No more purpose to live for, no more hope to look forward to, no more sense to my life. My life is a quest, and if it is not that, it is nothing. Once I meet God, my life will cease to be what it is meant to be: the search for God. I cannot meet him and go on living on earth. Let the darkness remain, let the longing remain, let the mystery remain.

And his running figure was lost far into the night.

This is a teaching as artistic as it is mystical, and as poetical as it is practical. Life is a search, and a search it must remain so long as it is life. There is faith in the searching, as we know the fullness of light awaits us at the end, and there is humility as we know much and we still have much to know. We can help one another by sharing with others what we know and letting them share with us what they in turn know. Let the mystery remain.

A MINI-POLAND IN ENGLAND

Immigration is helping the Churches. The drop in Church attendance is a matter of worry in Europe and America as it indicates a drop in active religious life and practice in traditionally Christian countries; and the influx of immigrants is already helping to revive dwindling congregations in many parishes in those countries. The London Catholic weekly *The Tablet,* 19 January 2008, p. 2, editorialises:

> "Disraeli is supposed to have coined the phrase 'lies, damned lies and statistics', which would, according to a recent report, be an apt comment on the accuracy of Catholic Mass attendance figures in England and Wales. Research by the Catholic sociologist, Dr Tony Spencer, indicates the true drop in figures over the last 10 years is more than half a million compared with a mere 72.000 in official figures based on annual returns from parishes. The results suggest a hidden but deep crisis in the native-born Catholic Church in these two countries, to which Dr Spencer applies the word 'alienation'."

If that is the diagnosis, this is now part of the remedy. The same weekly, on 6 October 2007, p. 12, carried an article under the headline "Immigrants from Goa bring the

Catholic community to bursting point":

> "Thousands of immigrants from the province of Goa in India are responsible for the phenomenal growth of an industrial city in England. About 9.000 Goans, whose ancestors were converted to Catholicism by Portuguese colonisers in the XVI century in India, have settled in the city of Swindon, attracted by work opportunities in an industrial environment.
>
> A massive immigration these last two or three years has resulted in a spectacular growth in the number of baptisms, first communions, and confirmations, as well as applications to Catholic schools which are now full to capacity. In the central Holy Cross parish, the parish priest Richard Twomey tells us, more than 3.000 faithful attend Mass each Sunday in the five Masses full to capacity.
>
> The Goan priest Francis Rosario travels to Swindon once a month from his parish in Mitcham, Surrey, to celebrate Mass in the Konkani language which is Goa's native language. There are also parishes of Goan immigrants in Reading, Maidenhead, and Wembley, the parish priest told us."

The sudden increase in new parishioners is such that it can also create problems, as the same weekly informs us. There are many Polish Catholic immigrants in Britain, and the Polish Cardinal Jozef Glemp in his Christmas message 2007 exhorted them as follows:

> "Poles can organise a mini-Poland in England and link it to their religious life. It is desirable to seek out Polish pastors and easy enough to find Polish church centres."

There is in fact a "Catholic Mission in England" from Poland since 1894 with a Polish vicar delegate and 219 parishes that depend on the Polish hierarchy and follow the pastoral programmes of the Polish bishops. *The Tablet* considers this "Polish Church" in England "an anomaly" which has no more sense today, and comments on the English cardinal's reaction to the Polish cardinal's proposal:

> "It will be necessary to handle with great diplomatic skill what looks like the beginning of a tug-of-war between the leadership of the Catholic Church in Poland and of the Catholic Church in England and Wales. Cardinal Cormac Murphy-O'Connor warned in an interview with a Polish news agency before Christmas that there was a danger that Polish immigrants, wanting to pray in their own language with their own priests and community activities, were creating a separate Church and thus were failing to integrate into the larger community. Judging by reported remarks of his opposite number in Warsaw, Cardinal Jozef Glemp, some kind of 'Church within a Church' was precisely what the Catholic bishops of Poland wanted.

> Cardinal Murphy-O'Connor is right to apply some of the lessons that Britain has painfully learned regarding other immigrant groups, particularly Pakistanis and Bangladeshis. The lesson is that if such groups insist on creating ghettos, physically or mentally, sooner or later a mood of resentment and alienation sets in that feeds on injustices, real or imagined. Community relations in Britain are not Cardinal Glemp's responsibility, but he is not entitled to disregard the consequences of a policy that could be harmful to British society. Polish cultural and linguistic preferences can be

accommodated in the short term, but in the long run this is not a good strategy.

Polish Catholics have an important contribution to make to English Catholic life, and that is why we welcome them from our heart; but if foreign Catholic hierarchies claim jurisdiction over every minority ethnic group of Catholics in England, the Church in England would become a house divided against itself." (*The Tablet,* 5 January 2008, p. 5)

From our point of view, which we have carefully built up in these pages, the controversy is clear, and we instinctively take sides with the English Catholic hierarchy. Immigrants do help us, and they do so by integrating themselves in our midst with mutual trust and natural spontaneity, by sharing with us their viewpoints and telling us their stories, by following their own beliefs, praying their prayers, celebrating their feasts, wearing their dresses, but doing so in harmony, in nearness, in fellowship, in unity with our own uses and customs and values that have now become their own. They bring the world to our door, and that is a blessing in culture and information, provided they approach us in trust and unity, in openness and brotherhood. No question of creating separate communities.

Immigrants do us a favour by existing among us. They universalise us. I often use the underground in Madrid, particularly Line 6 which is close to my residence and is favoured by immigrants as it also covers many of their residential areas. I travel surrounded by countries. It is a treat to look around and see faces and colours and gestures and expressions that draw the map of the world in the carriages of the train. This is a World Fair. Every trip is a luxury cruise, every wagon is a continent. I come out of the underground renovated and rejuvenated with the bath of cultures and countries I see and imagine in the faces round me and in the eyes that meet mine. Many Saturdays evening I go to the Berlin Park in East Madrid, and there *I* am the foreigner. All around me there are brown faces, short statures, musical lilts to the Spanish language. It is the meeting place for Peruvians with their games, their groups, their accent, their barbecues. By the side there is the Church of Our Lady of Guadalupe, Patroness of Mexico and of South America, one of the artistic churches in the capital. It is shaped as a tent. We all fit inside it.

BREAKING BOUNDARIES

Again monsoon time, now with myself on my bicycle along an open road between endless fields full of life and colour and music and birds. I am just enjoying a ride far from the city to rest my mind and feast my senses on the lush landscapes of nature at her best. Suddenly I stop my cycle and look intently to my right. A snake. A cobra. Half coiled, half erected on the shining grass in front of a low bush at the end of the field. And on the bush, a sparrow. I knew snakes did that to birds, and now I am seeing it. The cobra, with her hood fully spread and her split tongue flickering in the air, is looking murder at the bird; and the bird, caught in the mesmerising look of the reptile, is unable to move. The land freezes. I shake my arms and shout. The cobra turns in anger towards me. I am safe with my foot on the pedal ready to speed away. I turn the front wheel towards the scene. The cobra hisses its fury, lowers itself reluctantly to the ground, and slides into the grass. The bird finds its wings and flies into the sky. Nature breathes relief. I push the pedal and continue my contemplative ride on my cycle. Fear has been conquered. Fearlessness is what gives us wings.

A cobra was also seen one day climbing on Gandhi's shoulder while he sat in prayer in the open ground of

Harijan Ashram by the Sabarmati River in Ahmedabad. Gandhi went on praying unconcerned among the flutter all around him till the snake slid down and away peacefully. People said that, according to Indian tradition, that was a sign that made him into a *Chakravarti* Emperor. It was, in any case, an image and symbol of a moral quality that stands high in the list of Indian virtues: fearlessness *(abhaya)*. It is signified in the traditional gesture, often seen in pictures and statues, of the right hand raised and open vertically with its palm forward, and parallel fingers pointing to heaven. It means in body language "Do not fear". You have nothing to be afraid of from me. Or from anybody else or anything else, for that matter. This is my greeting to you, my wish for you, my blessing on you. *Abhaya-dan.* Gift of fearlessness. Do not fear.

Tagore in his autobiography narrates his early encounters with fear. When he was a small child in the large Tagore household, he was sometimes placed under the supervision of a servant for hours on end. The servant would place him in the middle of a large room in the stately mansion, draw round him a circle with chalk on the floor, and threaten him that if he stepped outside it, a monster would come and swallow him. Then he would leave. The frightened child did not dare cross the white circle and remained a lonesome prisoner in the phantom jail. A prisoner of fear. When, after hours, the servant came back and rubbed off the chalk, the child could step into the world again, though weakened and shaken by the frightening threat. When he grew and sensed the sting of the childhood experience, he wrote down the episode to exorcise its curse and recover strength.

In India we have precisely a unique festival which has something to do with this breaking free of boundaries. It symbolises, fosters and celebrates the conquest of fear in an ancient ceremony with a timeless interpretation. The king had selected a prize horse from his stables and had kept it, fed it, and pampered it for a whole year with full honours and luxurious care. Now, when the monsoon was over, when the labourers had finished their intensive yearly work at their fields with ploughing and sowing and watering and tending, and were free to join the king's army, the time had arrived for the ranks to be swollen with conscripts from the countryside, and the new army became ready for the winter campaign during the favourable months away from the heat and the rains. On the auspicious day of *Dassera*, the tenth day *(das* means "ten") of the bright half of the month Ashwin, round about September-October, the horse was set free, without rider or bridle, and the whole army followed its wanderings. The horse crossed the frontiers of the kingdom, galloped and cantered and frolicked and capered at will, and whatever new lands it stepped on were annexed to the crown. If there was no opposition, the conquest was peaceful, and if an army opposed its advance, the horse's army fought a war and ensured possession. The campaign lasted into the winter months, and horse and army returned victoriously home. The horse was then solemnly sacrificed to the gods in official thanksgiving and popular rejoicing. That was the day of The Sacrifice of The Horse *(Ashwamedha)* and The Crossing of Frontiers *(Simollanghan)*.

Apart from the war and the sacrifice, the teaching and the image stand in our minds. This is the chance to enlarge frontiers and widen characters. The frontiers of fear in our life mark the limits of our present personality, and, consequently and challengingly, signal to us the direction of our growth as persons. We, humans, have our territories subtly marked out in our conscience and in our behaviour. We feel safe and secure so long as we stick to what we instinctively know to be the boundaries of our character, our capability, our territory. In relationships, in work, in games, in sport, we know our familiar grounds, we sense our borders, and we quietly draw back when we feel uneasy and uncomfortable with new persons, new tasks, new situations next to the frontier where our territory ends. This is our common situation through the year. And now comes the call. The call to wake up, to develop, to grow, to break frontiers and conquer horizons; the challenge to let free the horse of our imagination on the auspicious day of the yearly feast, to garland it with the flowers of our enthusiasm and our faith, to brave new obstacles and explore new lands, to fight new fights and achieve new victories, to know that we can do better than we have done to date and we can reach farther than we have reached so far, and to pledge that we are now determined to take our chance in our hands and push for the new landscapes and new spaces that spread out in front of us and call us to new conquests. Routine, laziness, caution, fear keep us within a chalk boundary which we know to be false but we fear to transgress. The frontiers of fear are the directions of our expansion and development. The Festival of the Boundaries is the festival of growth. That is *Dassera, The Tenth Day.

The Tenth Day makes allusion to the nine days that precede it, or rather the Nine Nights *(Nav-ratri),* one of the loveliest festivals in India. Nine consecutive nights in which young women worship with dances and candles and clay vessels of sprouting grass the female partners of Brahma, Vishnu and Siva, that is Saraswati, Lakshmi and Parvati, asking for their blessings over themselves and over all their lives as virgins, brides, and mothers. Prayer for a good career, a good husband, a good family. They dance their prayers round and round through the hours of the night, they wake up early each of the nine days to carry to the temple their offerings and their longings, and then they come to class at the College, place their heads on their bent elbows on the desk, and sleep out peacefully the virginal fatigue of their past sleepless night. During my many years teaching mathematics at College, I never once woke up any of my girl students during the *Navratri* days while they slept peacefully in class after the nine sacred nights where they had placed their life with a prayer in the hands of God. Saraswati, goddess of learning, would help them through their exams. I only wondered, looking at them tenderly while I – with faked aloofness – explained theorem after theorem on the blackboard, what dreams those lovely girls were dreaming with their heads on their desks. *Navratri* is the festival that makes them women, and *Dassera* the festival that makes them grow. Ten days to celebrate. For life.

The Feast of the Boundaries is connected to the two essential virtues of no-violence and no-fear. We become violent because we are afraid. Insecurity generates fear, and fear breeds violence. The breaking of boundaries liberates us from fear, and fearlessness strengthens us towards non-violence. This is our tradition. This is Indian culture.

DEATH WITH CHOCOLATE

All fears come ultimately from death. Sickness speaks of mortality, partings foretell the final separation, failures breed finitude. All fears converge on the fear of death as the end of the known, the final reckoning, the suspense before eternity, and all draw from it their uneasiness, their unsettling, their threats. The image is not kindly either. The Reaper. The skeleton, the scythe, the skull. Not a pleasant visit to look forward to. Death is a taboo.

Here India has also something to share with the world. It is true that death is the ultimate equaliser as it deals with king and vassal alike, but the way different people look at it varies greatly, and it shapes differently the mentalities of those people and their lives. I have mentioned, when speaking about the Diwali festival, that Yama, the God of Death, is called The Supreme Guest because it always comes unannounced as a true guest should. But he is a guest! Not an enemy, not a calamity, not a threat. He is welcomed, honoured, looked after with care and devotion. And then, he is accompanied on his way out by the soul he came to fetch in his errand in joyful company. Karsandas Manek, Gujarati poet and mystic who honoured me with his friendship and autographed for me his book of religious poems *Ram, Taro Divado* (Your Lamp, Oh Rama!), which became my own

prayer-book for years, explained to me one of the poems
I specially loved in it. A doctor friend of his checked him
once after a giddy spell and told him he had suffered a
heart attack. He added, with a doctor's earnestness and
a friend's concern, that it was a serious one and the next
one could be fatal. Karsandas came home from the clinic
and, poet that he was, sat down and wrote at a stretch a
poem to God's messenger, The Angel of Death. It was not a
poet's imagination for one more poem, but a heart patient's
reaction after the doctor's diagnosis. That is why each line
of the poem rung true and carried conviction. No wonder
it had struck me. I learned it by heart and recited it often
to myself and to my public in lectures and talks. Here is it
in translation:

"God's messenger has shone in light,
an urgent message on his lips:
Roll up your tent, you pilgrim soul,
and leave the lush and fragrant fields!

Welcome to you, God's messenger!
Welcome to your commanding writ!
I roll up willingly my tent,
And leave the lush and fragrant fields.

No testament for me to write,
no last desires to express;
no wisdom words for me to utter,
no lost occasions to regret.

Nothing is hidden in my life,
no double dealings in my word;
I lived expecting you at each moment,
come, take me to the house of God."

Such were the deaths I witnessed in families close to
me, and I read about in biographies. C. Rajagopalachari,

one of the stalwarts of the Gandhian era and the first Indian Governor-General after Mountbatten, died at the age of 94. His doctor bent gently over his bed to speak in his ear and asked him how he felt. Rajaji, as he was universally and lovingly called, said clearly, "I am very happy", and gently passed away. The moment of death is the moment of truth. And he was happy.

A European friend of mine who lives in India and has studied Indian mores and has mixed with Indian society and has witnessed its many moods and customs and events and rites, likes to say, with a touch of black humour, that when someone in India comes to know that a friend is terminally ill, they go to visit them and tell them cheerfully in their bed, "Congratulations, my dear friend! What is this I hear about you? Fancy, you're breathing your last! Isn't it wonderful?" A bit exaggerated, to be sure, but it strikes the note. Death is not made a fuss of. Tagore, again, gave this poetical and tender image of death: a child is nursing at its mother's breast; milk has run out, and the mother gently moves the child away from that breast and brings it to the other. The child cries at being taken away from the source of its nourishment and thinking it is losing its vital support for ever; but the transit last only an instant, and soon the child is feeding again with renewed eagerness at the new source of life. Death is the brief interval between Mother Nature's two breasts. Two lives, and one tear in between. Thus says the poet. Maybe belief in reincarnation helps keep the peace before what is only one more death in the series of many that have gone before and that will follow; just as belief in one life, one death, one heaven, one hell once and for eternity, may heighten the tension of the moment and the anxiety before the one and only death. Count Karlfried Dürkheim narrates how a Christian missionary he met in Japan told him that his converts were all genuine and devout in their new faith and obediently followed all the customs and directives and practices they were taught; but he only complained that when it came to death, all his parishioners "went back to their heathen tradition and died the Japanese way". When the Count enquired from the priest what he meant by "the Japanese way", he explained that they died quietly, peacefully, unobtrusively, without any anxiety or fear, without sending for the priest or asking for blessings or submitting to special rites or reciting prayers. They just died in peace, and that was not, it would seem, what the good missionary had expected. This, once more, does not mean preferring one mentality to another, but watching reality all around us, affirming our own view and enriching it with the views of others. Kalelkar begins his book "Death, Our Closest Friend" with the words: "Death may cause pain as it brings separation, but not, of itself, fear. The fear aspect of death had been added by us: by some of us."

Swami Krishnanandji of Bhadran Ashram tells this story, again with a touch of humour before death, and with the expression of his own surprise at an extreme example of equanimity in a sudden trial. He went to visit a friend of his in Mumbai and was talking with him in his drawing room when, after a while, the friend's wife came with two cups, not of the traditional tea, but of hot chocolate which, she knew, was the favourite drink of the two friends. She left the tray on a low table before them, turned to leave the room, and then, suddenly and dramatically collapsed there itself on the spot. Both the men stood up, laid her down on the coach, called urgently a doctor who arrived at once, bent over her, examined her, straighten himself up, looked at the two men, shook his head, and declared her dead. A sudden massive heart attack had ended her life there and then. There was nothing to do. They both grieved with the shock, and, once the tragic end was absolutely certain, went to the phone to inform family and friends. Once all the people that had to be contacted were informed, the two friends sat down to wait for the comers in the drawing room as improvised funeral parlour. Then the husband spoke: "We have done all we had to do. Now we wait here for the people to come. Our two cups are still on the table untouched. Let us take our chocolate before it gets cold. It was her last service to us." And in silence they drank their cocoa still warm.

GLIBLY

Karma is another word gifted by India to the world. A very successful gift indeed. Even in the west, persons and events and places and smells have, nowadays, or bring with them, good karma or bad karma or positive karma or negative karma or no karma at all or are full of karma or fit with each other's karma or fight against each other's karma or vibrate with karma or die of karma. It's karma all round and for everybody every time, and it explains why some things go right and some wrong without apparent reason, why we succeed without trying or fail after striving, why we at any moment are sad or happy, healthy or sick, alive or dead. A universal word.

Originally *kar* is just "hand" in Sanskrit, and *karma* is whatever the hand does by way of work, gesture, or action. The person's record of all their actions in thought, word, or deed is the sum of their karma, and this "weight" of karma is what defines the moral status of the person at the moment, and as such determines what is to happen to it in reward or punishment. A "good" karma makes for good luck and good health and success in life in general, while a "bad" karma is responsible for failure, sickness and death. More important still, the quality and measure of karma at the moment of death determines the quality of the new birth in the next incarnation. Good karma will bring a noble birth in a good family with good life conditions, while bad karma will mean a low birth in poverty and squalor. This is a very popular explanation of a most vexing situation, that is, the difference in birth for the child, from a prosperous and healthy family in an advanced society with bright prospects in life, to an indigent and sick family in a desolate land with just a few months to live. The karma of the last birth would account for the difference. Simple solution to an otherwise perplexing question.

Karma, more generally, is an attempt to understand, to explain, to come to terms with the riddle of human life with its ups and downs, its successes and failures, its joys and sorrows, and chiefly with the main query and sheer mystery of humans on earth: suffering. Why is there so much suffering in human life, why is there so much suffering in my own life, why should this happen to me, why should it happen now, why should it happen at all? All ages and all races, all philosophies and all religions, all sages and all simple people have faced the riddle of riddles, the tears of the mother before her sick child, the distress of failure and the despair of depression, the anguish of the human heart before a bond of love that breaks itself and breaks with it the hearts it once united, the tragedy in a family, the bewilderment of humankind before earthquakes and floods and volcanoes and tornadoes, the agony of terminal cancer, the parting of death. Why, why, why? Why to me, why now, why at all? The utmost delicacy and humility are called for when we deal with this, the deepest and darkest reality of the human existence on earth, and, on the other hand, the utmost sincerity and authenticity are also required to heal the wounds instead of deepening them with cheap answers and routine explanations. The suffering of the human heart is too real and too raw in the flesh to be dealt with superficially with easy stereotypes and trite formulas. We do not play with blood.

I once conducted a thirty-day continuous Spiritual Retreat or Meditation Camp in silence and prayer on the lovely slopes of the Western Ghats in Khandala, Maharashtra, for a group of young Indian Jesuits who were preparing themselves for their immediate work in schools and parishes. While the experience proved an uplifting one for most of them, there was one fine young man who had come to the Camp when he was under a heavy cloud of family problems, vocational uncertainties and existential doubts, and for whom the month-long retreat in solitude and self-examination proved an unremitting test of mental perplexity, spiritual dryness, and plain moral endurance. When the ordeal was over and he took leave of me, we went gently together over his whole painful experience, and he told me: "One thing I have learned in this drawn out month: never for the rest of my life will I speak glibly about suffering." I told him: "Maybe you are the one that has profited most by this experience. And you have helped me too. I've gone through the test with you and I'll treasure its lesson. If you allow me, I'll mention your conclusion to others without mentioning your name. And I will quote your word as it has stuck in my mind: glibly."

It is in this spirit of deep respect and gentle delicacy that I will now briefly summarise the teaching of the main religions in the world about suffering. The fact that there are different explanations alerts us to the reality that none of them is conclusive, and the sincerity and humility of each consideration helps us find the solace that fits with our own mentality in our sufferings, as also the ways to accompany others in theirs. A brief summary of each view can do justice to none, but the quick survey of all can help to hold them together before our mind for clarity and perspective.

This can prove a meaningful exercise in the ecumenical approach adopted in this book, namely the steadfastness to hold to one's own tradition and the readiness to understand those of others.

Hinduism. Our karma, that is the sum total of our actions in past incarnations and in our present life to date, is responsible for whatever happens to us in our life, whether pleasant or unpleasant, from birth to death. Morally good past actions effect rewarding results in body and mind, and morally bad actions bring us suffering sooner or later. Our past errors have to be paid for with actual sufferings as their penance, our misdeeds have to be atoned for, and our bad karma has to be burned in the fire of mental or bodily pain. Thus, in the midst of the strongest suffering we have the consolation to know that we are paying our debt, as we rightfully and inexorably have to do, and the sooner we pay our debt, the better it is. This is also a strong motivation to avoid immoral actions in the future.

Brahmanism. Suffering and joy are in fact not real, but are only the illusion caused by the veil of Maya, our senses, our limited understanding, our narrow self. The true Self is above all such illusory sensations, and in the realisation of that supreme truth there is peace. Illumination, enlightenment and spiritual awakening obtained through systematic meditation and ascetical practices lead us to the true vision that places us above and beyond the vicissitudes of sensorial perception in the ego-less equilibrium of self-realisation.

Buddhism. There is suffering; the cause of suffering is desire; the remedy of suffering is the suppressing of desire. Rather than "desire", the translation of the Buddha's principle should be "craving", that is, inordinate desire. Such a yearning for material gains upsets the inner balance of the soul and causes suffering. If the desired object is not obtained, the mind suffers; and if the desired object is obtained, the mind instantly yearns for a higher one and the spiral soars into unavoidable misery. Right conduct in thought, word and deed allays desire and avoids suffering. Detachment and compassion are the key to inner peace.

Jainism. We are caught in the cycle of reincarnations, and our salvation lies in escaping from it. Suffering, accepted as it comes to us in life, shortens the cycle. But we can do more. We can add on our own voluntary penances and hardships, prayer and fasting, vows and vigils that will cut our bonds, speed us on our way, and accelerate liberation. Self-restraint is the way.

Zoroastrianism. There is only one God but two principles or rather mentalities, one good and one evil, which are responsible for the corresponding inclinations in humans. The choice is within us with the consequences it entails. Calamities of nature are ethically neutral. Asceticism is rejected, as all creation is good and we honour its Creator by using it and enjoying it. Suffering is just to be born when it overtakes us, and gently avoided as far as we can, while we make the best of the good things of life which is God's gift to us.

Taoism. Joy and pain are two sides of the same coin, and as we take one, we must inevitable take the other. The moment we say "beauty" we have created "ugliness", as one can exist and be perceived only in contrast to the other. There is no summit without a valley, no light without darkness, no heat without cold, no virtue without vice, no rejoicing without suffering. Reality is one of a piece, and each couple of opposites has to be taken as an inseparable unity and accepted as such. Yin and Yang.

Confucianism. The purpose of our existence is for us to live a noble and righteous life in family and society with obedience to the rules, respect to our elders, and veneration of our ancestors. We achieve that by making reality the names we receive as sons and daughters, parents and citizens, masters and servants, so that the son has to be a good son and the father a true father. An upright character and steadfastness of purpose is the condition for such a life. This character is shaped and strengthened in the crucible of suffering, which makes us mature into better persons and helps us better to understand ourselves and to deal with others.

Animism. We are part of nature with all its rhythms and cycles and seasons and tides, and with it we recognise in ourselves the succession of moods and temper, of high and low, of far and near, of pain and joy that mark the throes and the pulse of creation. We share in the processes of life and growth with all the vicissitudes and changes they entail. Any injure to nature brings back suffering, not only in human beings, not only in animals and plants, but in each being that exists and is part of the cosmic existence as land and water and heaven and earth. The flower falls that the fruit may ripen.

Islam. Faith is the first pillar of Islam, and submission to the will of God its first practical consequence. The will of God rules the course of the planets in heaven and the lives of humans on earth. Our fulfilment as God's creatures lies in acknowledging and embracing his most holy will in the circumstances that surround us and in the events that befall us. It is not for us to question the divine will, but to accept it with joy and gratitude whatever its biddings. God never sends us sufferings without a purpose, and through them makes us worthier as believers and faithful.

Judaism. Suffering is fundamentally God's punishment for the infidelities of his people. He leads his Chosen People through desert and conquest into the Holy Land with the hope of the coming Messiah, decrees the laws they have to obey in order to ensure his blessings, and considers as a breach of contract and a threat to his historical designs on humankind any personal infraction of his rules that, consequently, has to be corrected immediately with due chastisement for the good of all.

Christianity. God's will, again, has to be accepted without questioning as it decrees the place and family and circumstances into which we are born and all that happens to us later in life for good or evil. Often it is human freedom that is the immediate cause of suffering. Also, suffering in this life ensures higher reward in the next, and "the outcome of our sufferings is eternal glory" (2 Corinthians 4:17). To this is added the redemptive aspect of our suffering, as Jesus died on the cross for the redemption of humankind, and our own sufferings now unite with his to "complete Christ's sufferings" (Colossians 1:24), thus giving a social dimension to our trials on earth.

We now appreciate the historical effort men and women have made throughout the ages, each from their own standpoint in time and culture, to understand in some way this riddle of riddles in human existence, and we are helped by their sincerity, their striving, and their light. We also learn from here how to console meaningfully a friend from a different religious persuasion from ours when sorrow visits them in their families or in their spirit, and they seek solace the way they know and makes sense to them. We know their feelings under grief and we will respect their interpretation of it.

One thing, in conclusion, stands out clearly after this

brief survey, and that is that human suffering has always been and will always remain a mystery, and as such is to be accepted, revered, gently avoided as far as possible, and duly embraced when it falls upon us as part of our mortal condition on earth and our human destiny for ever. And never, never, never to speak glibly about it.

INDRA'S NET

India is proud of the fact that it was an Indian botanist, Jagdis Chandra Bose, that, at the beginning of last century, drew the world's attention to the fact that plants have sensation, feelings, moods, feel hurt, suffer, experience fear, relief, joy. And Jainism had from time immemorial classified beings as "one-sensed", like air, water, fire, earth, plants which have only the sense of touch; "two-sensed" like insects that add the sense of taste; "three-sensed" as snails with smell; "four-sensed" with sight as a butterfly; and "five-sensed" like humans and beasts with hearing. The classification looks naïve, but the insight is powerful. All beings are nature. All are alive. All are born and grow and feel and react and form part of the cosmic universe that embraces all beings in the unity of creation. Ecology is a modern term, and ecological measures and policies in our legislation and in our behaviour, our homes, our roads, our fields, our mountains, our trees and our food are of recent application; but the philosophical basis for this latest development of human awareness and its spiritual dimension in all its wide reach is the acknowledgment that nature is alive, and that conviction was reached and verbalised in India much before the term "ecology" was coined by the Greens. We respect nature, not in order to preserve egoistically its treasures for ourselves, but because in its own way it is alive, feels, and grows, and we respect, reverence, and worship life in all its forms. This is the heart of ecology.

Rivers and seas, mountains and valleys, deserts and forests, fields and trees, birds and cattle and fish are to be protected, cared for, nursed because of themselves   and of their dignity, their beauty, their life. There is an old Sanskrit prayer to be said on getting up in the morning, in which we ask for pardon from Mother Earth for stepping on her. She does not mind our stepping on her, on the contrary, she loves our touch and cradles our step, but she does suffer when we abuse her and pollute her and hurt her without care. The earth shakes and wails in the continued creation of its nuclear depths; the oceans swell and heave in the restlessness of their abysmal power; the winds and the storms embrace the earth with the swift currents of their primeval might. Water caresses our bodies, outside and inside as bath and as drink; fire warms our members and cooks our food; air is all the time all around us, fills our lungs and gives life to our life in our own blood. Atmospheric pollution is a sin against nature and a sin against blood. We have to keep our surroundings holy.

Tourists in India, particularly along some of the north-western states, if they get up early enough to walk the streets before the sun climbs high and makes the daily wanderings of holy monks and nuns with bare feet impossible on the steaming asphalt, will be lucky to watch their white figures sliding along the pavement with quick steps and lowered eyes. The tourist will notice that those saintly men and women all wear a small oblong piece of spotless clean white clothing across their mouths fixed with slender ribbons to their ears. The tourist guide will then explain to their charges that those are Jain monks and nuns who profess a deep respect for all kind of life and take actually a vow of non-violence as one of their five religious vows, and so, in order to save themselves from the untoward mishap of swallowing an insect, even if unawares, place that piece of cloth before their mouths for the protection of all flying insects and creatures of the air. This is fine, no doubt, but there is more to it than the tourist guide knows, and the real meaning and function of the white cloth is quite another. Jain monks and nuns are not so naïve and careless as to go on swallowing flies as they walk in the open. The cloth is for something else. We have just seen that the air is alive. It has the sense of touch. It feels. It can be hurt. It is highly sensitive to strokes and blows. When we speak we can hurt the air. A plosive "p" or even "b" at the beginning of a word in idiomatic English pronunciation that strikes its consonants as cannon shots is a veritable explosion against the air in front of us. It is punching and stabbing a living being. It is violence. To avoid that comes the little piece of cloth that stops the outgoing blow, breaks its speed, stops its violence, filters its current. And conversation can harmlessly be conducted across the protective veil. Reverence to nature. Or, in Franciscan language, respect for Brother Air.

Once I gave a talk to a group of Jain nuns who sat on the ground in front of me so that I was facing a design of clean white rectangles spread out before my sight at regular intervals from face to face in the large hall. I had no veil, bless my pagan soul, though it was I that was doing most of the talking and recklessly hammering the air away, but their sanctity and modesty made up for my brazen forwardness in the enlightened morning. We struck an instant friendship, we laughed and joked, we thought and shared, we questioned and left questions hanging in the air, and we truly became one in mind and in feeling. At one moment in the proceedings I told them: "I will not cease till I see your smiles coming out of your cloth at the sides!" That did it. The white clothes vibrated with joy. Though no one removed it from her mouth. They knew better than that. One of them went stealthily out, came back unobtrusively, approached me and then handed me a small white cloth with its side ribbons for my use. I put it on among the general rejoicing, and then it was my smile that burst the rectangular veil and shook the atmosphere around. I don't know whether my words remained intelligible any longer across the white border, but our hearts did meet and our souls vibrated together. That day Brother Air became truly a part of the meeting and infused us all with its own life. And I became an Honorary Jain for a day.

Every river is sacred. Not only the Ganges. Every river is a Mother of Peoples *(Lokmata)*, as goes the title of the masterful book of Kakasaheb Kalelkar in which he artistically weaves the history of India along the length of her rivers. The Narmada River, or The Ganges of The West, is, since the sixth century, the scene of an ecological pilgrimage through fields and forests, that starts at its source in Amarkant, reaches its mouth at Bharuch, crosses the river at that point only, and goes back on the other side till the source again, thus covering sixteen hundred miles keeping always the river on the right. Festival of nature, spirit, water, and land.

Gandhi's spinning wheel was an ecological symbol. Shri Krishna is close to nature with his peacock feather, his cows, his conch-shell, his flute. When Prime Minister Jawaharlal Nehru asked Vinoba Bhave how he could rule India best, the sage advised him: "Play the flute one hour every day." Our ancient books contain the allegory of Indra's Net that weaves the whole cosmos together with the discovery of one pearl in each knot of the web and the whole universe reflected in each pearl.

"The celestial Jewel Net of Kanishka, or Indra, god of gods and emperor of emperors, is called the Net of Indra. This imperial net is made of jewels: because the jewels are clear, they reflect each other's images, appearing in each other's reflections upon reflections without end, all appearing at once in one jewel, and in each one it is so – ultimately there is no going or coming.

If you sit in one jewel then you are sitting in all jewels in every direction, multiplied over and over. Why? Because in one jewel there are all the jewels. If there is one jewel in all jewels, then you are sitting in all jewels too. And the reverse applies to the totality if you follow the same reasoning. Since in one jewel you go into all the jewels without leaving this one jewel, so in all jewels you enter one jewel without leaving this one jewel." (Avatamsaka Sutra in "Buddhism and Ecology", Martine Batchelor and Kerry Brown, p. 11)

Galactic net of the totality of creation in the totality of the cosmos from the smallest atom to the most remote confines of the universe. Every knot is a pearl. A precious pearl of infinite value and transcendent beauty. A pearl different from all pearls, and each pearl living in all the other pearls. Each pearl reflects all other pearls in the net in all their totality and identity, and each pearl in turn is reflected in its totality and identity on all the other pearls in the net. We are all connected. Who could number the reflections, the sparkles, the iridescence, the glitter, the twinkling lights, the intertwining trajectories, the design of the whole universe on the delicate surface of each pearl! If you see one, you see all, and contemplating all you reduce them all to one. We are kin to all beings. From a particle of cosmic dust to the living image of the king of creation we are all united in light and distance, in value and purpose, in dignity and love. Cosmic parable. Environmental challenge. Web of webs. Digital dream. Ecological dream.

INDIA'S SECRET

At the beginning of my long stay in India I once met a 90 year old yogi who showed me joyfully all the wonders of his masterful breathing. His breast was naked, with only the signature of his Brahmin thread etched on his light bronze shining skin from left shoulder to right side, and it showed, in its firmness and suppleness, the effect of the discipline of a true professional of breathing. He emptied his breast, he made it swell, he played one lung against the other, he made waves with his ribs, he thinned out, he filled up, he hardened, he softened. He could remain without breathing longer than an Egyptian mummy. Then he let out the air in a gust of wind and laughed heartily as a mischievous child. It was an entertaining and enlightening show of what one can do with life's most monotonous and routine exercise. And his energy and his vitality at 90 testified to the efficacy of his training.

At the end of his demonstration, he came close to me with a meaningful look in his eyes, lowered his voice to a conspiratorial whisper and told me in my ear: "This is India's secret. Not only for the health of the body, but of the mind also. Breathing. And, more than that, conscious breathing which is the real thing and you will have to learn. Discover it and be happy. And then tell others about it..., though they will not believe you." And he laughed out loudly again.

Later in my Indian years I attended a ten-day *Vipassana* course with Shri Swaminarayan Goenka in his *Dammagiri* institution at Igatpuri. It was an unforgettable experience. *Vipassana* is based on *Annapanna* or Conscious Breathing, and aims at the integration of our bodily sensations into the full awareness of the present moment, thus achieving integral peace, spiritual concentration, and continued wellbeing. Goenkaji had inherited the ancient practice from his master U Ba Khin (1899-1971) who had rescued it from Buddhist tradition and had popularised it in Myanmar (Burma). His was the saying that summarised the teaching: "Man's best friend is his nose." Woman's best friend is her nose. There is no question here of improving one's breathing, of deepening, controlling, directing, mastering the ins and outs of air in our lungs. All that is fine and can be done with fruit – and that was what the yogi had shown; but this is not the real point – as the yogi himself had expressly said. The point here is only and significantly to be aware of our breathing, to sense it, to accompany it. To notice the gentle influx of air through our nose.

Inside our nostrils grow a few short, stray, delicate hairs that seem to us superfluous and obnoxious, and that we even trim with blunt scissors not to hurt the sensitive skin. But those little hairs are not there by mistake, and that zone is not oversensitive without a reason. We should leave those hairs in their place, neat and clean, as they are the sentries that welcome the incoming guests and notify us of their arrival so that we may come out to greet them when they reach us in their aerial visit. The air, the oxygen, the breath. The ambassadors of life. Our nostrils are the reception hall in the palace of our body. That is why they are so delicate, so tender, so sensitive, so embellished with plush velvet on their walls and quiet luxury in their depths.

From there we follow the gentle, soft, relaxing, vivifying flow of the life-giving breeze through the tissues of our body and the intimacy of our inmost being. There is no question of imagining passages or describing itineraries, but just following the spreading of wellbeing as our organs welcome the oxygen and come to life with it. Breathing in and breathing out.

Breathing goes on in us while walking or standing, while eating or drinking, while working or resting, while talking and praying, and this continuous thread of conscious breathing through every hour of the day and every day of our lives becomes the key to our integration and the mainstay of our happiness. Conscious breathing unwinds the body, pacifies the mind, quietens the senses, ushers in wellbeing. In fact, books are being written and manuals are being multiplied to popularise conscious breathing among all kinds of people and offices from management to sports. A cartoon in *The New Yorker* highlighted the fashion by depicting a high executive in his Manhattan suite with wide windows on the crenellated skyline, four telephones ringing on his table, and the computer screen flickering in front of him while he, in his impeccable three-piece suit and dark tie, had awkwardly crossed his legs on the floor, had closed his eyes, placed his fingers in imitation of the Buddha's hands, and from his lips flew the repeated sacred formula, *Hari Om, Hari Om, Hari Om...* East meets West at last.

Everybody, East or West, knows about India's great gift to the world, the Buddha. His princely status, his protected childhood, his discovery of suffering in a beggar, a sick man, an old man, a dead body, his awakening, his flight from the palace, his enlightenment, his Eightfold Path, his disciples, his death, his Nirvana. Yet few seem to know that the core of the Buddha's teaching is precisely the doctrine and practice of conscious breathing, and the most famous among the writings emanating from him is the ancient *Anna-panna-sati Sutra,* or "Canon *(sutra)* of The Consciousness *(sati)* of Breathing In *(anna)* and Breathing Out *(panna)*". I quote here the Canon and the solemn occasion of its proclamation from the recent and inspiring biography of the Buddha by Thich Nhat Hahn:

> "When the full moon day of Kattika arrived, *kumudi* flowers were blossoming everywhere. Because the *kumudi,* a white lotus, always blossomed at the same time each year, the full moon day of Kattika was called Kumudi Day. That evening the Buddha and his three thousand disciples sat beneath the radiant full moon. The delicate fragrance of lotus flowers drifted up from the lake. The monks and nuns sat silently as the Buddha looked out over the community and praised them for their diligence. The Buddha used this special occasion to deliver the 'Sutra on the Full Awareness of Breathing'.
>
> Of course, every monk and nun present had been taught the method of the awareness of breathing. But this was the first time that most of them had an opportunity to hear this teaching directly from the Buddha. This was also the first time the Buddha compiled and summarised all his previous teachings on the awareness of breathing. Venerable Ananda listened intently, knowing that this sutra would be an important one to transmit to all the sangha's centres. The Buddha delivered the sermon:
>
> 'Bhikkhus and Bhikkhunis, the method of the Full Awareness of Breathing, if developed and practised continuously, will bring great rewards and advantages, and will give rise to Understanding and Liberation. The practice is as follows:

Breathing in as a short breath, I know I am breathing in as a short breath. Breathing out as a short breath, I know I am breathing out as a short breath.

Breathing in, I am aware of my whole body. Breathing out, I am aware of my whole body.

I am breathing in and making my whole body calm and at peace. I am breathing out and making my whole body calm and at peace.

I am breathing in and feeling joyful. I am breathing out and feeling joyful.

I am breathing in and feeling happy. I am breathing out and feeling happy.

I am breathing in and am aware of the activities of the mind in me. I am breathing out and am aware of the activities of the mind in me.

I am breathing in and making the activities of the mind in me, calmed and at peace. I am breathing out and making the activities of the mind in me, calmed and at peace.

I am breathing in and am aware of my mind. I am breathing out and am aware of my mind.

I am breathing in and making my mind happy and at peace. I am breathing out and making my mind happy and at peace.

I am breathing in and concentrating my mind. I am breathing out and concentrating my mind.

I am breathing in and liberating my mind. I am breathing out and liberating my mind.

I am breathing in and contemplating liberation. I am breathing out and contemplating liberation.

I am breathing in and contemplating letting go. I am breathing out and contemplating letting go.'

So taught the Buddha how to observe deeply the body, feelings, mind, and objects of mind through conscious breathing. Three thousand monks and nuns joyously received the Buddha's teaching that night beneath the light of the full moon." (Thich Nhat Hahn, Old Path White Clouds, p. 375)

The Buddha observed that his son, Rahula, who had followed him in his renunciation, was getting negligent and distracted in his observances, and asked him, "Rahula, are you keeping mindfulness of your breath?", and when Rahula lowered his head in answer, the Buddha instructed him: "To dwell in mindfulness, you must continue to observe your breath. Observe your breath, and your mind will not become dispersed. Breathing in, you are aware that you are breathing in. Breathing out, you are aware that you are breathing out. With just one breath, you can attain awakening." (p. 320)

When the Buddha's father, King Suddhodana, was in his deathbed in Kapilavatthu, the Buddha went to his side, sat down by the bed, took the king's hand in his own and told his father: "Father, please, breathe gently and slowly. Smile. Nothing is more important than your breath at this moment. Nanda, Ananda, Rahula, Anuruddha, and I will breathe together with you." The king smiled and began to follow his breath. After a while he closed his eyes and passed away from this life. Queen Gotami and Yashodhara (the Buddha's mother and wife) began to cry. The Buddha told them to follow their breathing." (p. 287)

Later in the book, when the author Thich Nhat Hahn comes to the death of the Buddha himself, he leaves a blank space and prints the request: "Reader, please put your book down here and breathe lightly for a few minutes before continuing." (p. 560)

This is the Buddha's teaching, this is his disciples' practice, this is India's secret. India, indeed, has kept her secret in the cleverest and safest way: she has protected the secret by making it an open secret. She has told everybody so that nobody may pay attention, she has unveiled the treasure so that nobody may search for it, she has placed the product in the market so that nobody may buy it. But it is there for the world to see, to appreciate, to embrace. A practice anybody can undertake at any age and from any background. A universal blessing. A unifying exercise. Conscious breathing is the Indian way to peace of body and mind. A peace that today is more necessary than ever.

THE GIANT WAKES UP

When I arrived in India with the mission to start a University College in Ahmedabad, for which purpose I chose to graduate in mathematics, I was recommended the then Madras University for the course, and I had full opportunity to witness to and to profit by the mathematical prowess of staff and students in the exclusive Honours Course that was the pride and glory of the University. The BA-MA syllabus was the same as the standard course, but the "honours" part of it added the sting of a final examination of ten three-hour written papers at the end which covered all the matter of all the courses studied in all the years, thus requiring a feat of memory, comprehension, and readiness hardly thinkable outside the mathematical tradition in South India. Besides, higher percentages were required for passing and for class, and a first class could not be obtained except by answering one of the "starred questions" that would baffle a seasoned researcher. Worst of all, if one failed the exam, there was no repetition for life, a condition that lead to the highest tension before the ultimate test.

The only relief in that dismal horizon was the option each paper offered. Ten questions with the heading "Write any seven" faced us at every exam, and the first task in the three hours of the test was to find out which seven would prove more amenable to our knowledge of the subject. When coming out of the examination hall in the famed Marine Drive of Chennai on the first day of our ordeal, I asked a companion of mine, C.S. Seshadri, how had he fared in the first paper. He answered nonchalantly: "I took the paper, answered in detail the ten questions in their order, and then I went back and wrote at the head of the first sheet: 'Correct any seven'. That'll ease their job."

That was the kind of student in that kind of atmosphere. I've said that South India was a land of mathematical tradition, and my experience confirmed what history already knew. Srinivasa Ramanujan was a Tamil Brahmin with a mathematical genius and no university education at the beginning of last century. He didn't know many elementary results, while he discovered and proved highly sophisticated theorems. G.H. Hardy was the English mathematician who introduced rigour in modern mathematics "with the fervour of a missionary preaching to cannibals" as he himself said, and it was he that recognised Ramanujan's genius and invited him to England as his patron and friend. He often expressed his frustration, as, every time he tried to teach Ramanujan some standard textbook formula needed for some demonstration, Ramanujan would burst out with an avalanche of original discoveries that flooded the blackboard and drowned the attempt at classroom education. Ramanujan fell sick during his stay in London and had to be hospitalised. Hardy went to visit him, greeted him and sat down by the side of his hospital bed. The stiff Englishman and the shy Indian could converse gloriously on mathematical matters, but did not have much to share by way of small talk. Hardy made an offhand remark, and his narrative of the exchange that followed it is a treasured anecdote in mathematical circles. Hardy begins:

- Well, it's the first time I come to a hospital.
- How did you come?
- I hailed a taxicab.
- Did you notice its plate number?
- Well, yes, I did. We deal in numbers after all, don't we?
- That's why I asked you. But tell me, was it any interesting number?
- Oh, no, not at all. Not a perfect square or a prime or a palindrome. In fact it was quite a dull number without anything special about it. I only hope this was not any bad omen for us.
- Oh no, not at all. But what was the number, anyhow? That is, if you remember it.
- Yes, yes. Wait…, it was 1729.
- What? 1729? And you say it is not an interesting number?
- Well, I don't see anything particular about it at all.
- But don't you see…, don't you realise…, don't you recall that 1729 is… the smallest positive integer… that can be expressed… as a sum of two cubes… in two different ways!!!
- Ah, yes, of course, of course. How silly of me not to have noticed it.

1729 is today called Ramanujan's Number, and quite a few characteristic properties of it have been found – apart from being the sum of two cubes in two different ways. In fact Hardy said that every positive integer was Ramanujan's personal friend. It is this personal friendship with numbers that is a trait of the Indian mathematical genius, and has traditionally helped calculation and computation from buying vegetables in the market place to obtaining technical formulae in the laboratory. Indian students in traditional villages learned the multiplication tables, not just up to 10, as children over the world do, but up to 40, and not only of integers, but of halves, so that, just as we can say "two times three is six", they could as quickly say "two-and-a-half times three-and-a-half is eight seventy-five", which, of course, I've had to work out on my hand calculator. These "half tables" were called "Cheating Tables" as their mastery ensured favourable business dealings in the trade. They also helped instant understanding of the mathematical lattice that is at the heart of every science.

This algebraic gift of the Indian mind has now effortlessly translated into computer skills with their algorisms and their programmes, their hardware and their software. India is overtaking cybernetic world powers and coming to the front in the international scene of business and industry. There is a climate of growth in the country that has swept through the land in a new spirit of work and efficiency, of imagination and creativity, of job dedication and financial success. All economic indexes are shooting upwards in India. There is nothing like the sense of conscious wellbeing and contagious euphoria in a country that wakes up to a new age of efficiency and excellence, and finds itself in the advancing frontiers of technology and enterprise, and anybody who visits the country can sense it now. The giant is on the move.

And there is more than that. There is not just question of competition in business, but of looking up to size up situations that had been taken for granted, measuring levels of fulfilment and satisfaction – or dissatisfaction – all around, realising that not everything is as wonderful in affluent societies as one had been led to think at the beginning, and waking up to the fact that one's own heritage can contribute to greater happiness and higher living than at present obtain in the West.

"Asians are shocked by the scale and depth of social and economic problems that have afflicted many Western societies. In North America, societies are troubled by the relative breakdown of the family as an institution, the plague of drug addiction and its attendant problems, including crime, the persistence of ghettos, and the perception that there has been a decline in ethical standards.

Asians are troubled by the addiction of Europeans to their social security nets despite the clear evidence that these nets now hold down their societies and have created a sense of gloom about long-term economic prospects. The American Bureau of the Budget recently forecast that for an American infant born at the beginning of the twenty-first century, the tax requirement to pay for existing programmes will be 82 percent of his lifetime earnings. This figure is obviously unsupportable. In previous decades, when East Asians visited North America and Western Europe, they envied the high standards of living and better quality of life in those societies. Today, though the high standards of living remain in the West, Asians no longer consider these societies as their role models. They are beginning to believe that they can attempt something different. This kind of mental horizon never existed in Asian minds until recently. It reveals the new confidence of Asian themselves.

The growing realisation among East Asians that they can match, if not better, other cultures or societies has led to an explosion of confidence." (Mahbubani, p. 28)

BRAHMINS, MULLAS AND PADRES

India is often referred to as "the largest democracy in the world", and the definition is right. It is not only the largest, but it is working, which is more important, and which cannot be said, unfortunately, of even smaller democracies elsewhere in the world, some of which are so only in name. There is the vast land, there are the millions, there are the regions and the traditions, there are different religions and languages, there is illiteracy and there is – inevitably – corruption and – occasionally – violence, but through it all and with it all there is a sense of belonging together, of a common destiny, of purpose and endeavour, of history and future, of faith and confidence that is shaping the country into a newborn power with all the freshness of the awakening and all the strength of a new dawn in history.

Democracy caught early in India because India was prepared for it. Here again words lead us in our search. Ancient Sanskrit contains the word *Gan-rajya* which literally means People's Rule, much before Athens would give us the word *demo-cracy* which means exactly the same in Greek. And if the word existed, that means that the spirit existed too. It was the time of emperors, but the great Emperors of India like Ashoka, Akbar, Vikramaditya, were known to encourage *Nagar Charcha* or Town Discussion to ascertain the will of the people, and to invite international scholars to discuss in public the issues of the times. In the Red Fort of Fatehpur Sikri, the capital Akbar built for himself at the peak of his power, the tourist is shown a strange structure which served a very particular purpose. It is a square hall with tall bare walls and closed ceiling. Midway up the walls there are four equal and independent balconies forming a square, each one with its own access door from the inside of the palace. One balcony was, of course, reserved for the Emperor and his ministers. In the balcony to his left sat the sadhus and Brahmins that represented the Hindu religion, to his right sat the mullas and maulvis of Islam, and in from the Jesuit missionaries or Padres that had recently arrived in the country in the name of Christianity. We know the names of this last delegation. They were Rudolf Acquaviva, Francis Henriques, and Jerome Xavier, nephew of St Francis Xavier, Catholic patron saint of India buried in Goa, whose name echoes in India today in Xavier's schools and Xavier's colleges throughout the land. The representatives of the three great religions exposed their views and sought consensus from wall to wall while the Emperor listened from his balcony, and people sat down on the floor watching the proceedings – with craned necks we suppose – and being educated in mutual respect and coexistence. Religion was then and has remained an important issue in the life of any country, and Akbar sought airing of views and popular understanding in its theory and its practice as the main basis for peace in his empire. He was ecumenical before his time.

India has had many capitals through history, and has today flourishing mega-cities along its landscape, but its heart has always remained in its villages. And its villages have been traditionally ruled by the *Gram Panchayat* or

Village Council of Five, recognised even today by India's constitution. The word *punch* (English spelling of *panch*) – and I will not miss my chance to establish another verbal link between East and West – is not unknown in Britain, though few today may recall its origin. "Punch" in English is a drink made of the mixture of five elements, usually water, juice, spices, wine, rum; and *punch* in Hindi *(panchayat)* means "Rule of Five". As simple as that. The spices in the drink are the specific Indian contribution, greatly enhancing the value of the mixture. The *Gram Panchayat* is the Village Council made up of five elders who rule the village in its laws and its customs, its quarrels and its frictions, its droughts and its floods. Popular rule. The number of five members can now be expanded and the procedures resemble those of any democratically elected body, but the tradition and the history, the spirit and the memories of the *Panchayati Raj* or Rule By The People ennoble the actual governing body and help its running in the present by reminding us of its past.

These old institutions explain the quick acceptance and wide success of democracy in India as the largest democracy in the world. The spirit was there, and the form has settled naturally on it. We certainly have something to contribute to the actual political status of the world with our quiet practice and long understanding.

A CRICKET MATCH

This has been a cursory review of what one particular Eastern culture can contribute to a typical Western culture, with a view to level out the scales and set the meeting of cultures on its proper balance. There is not one side that gives and one that receives. Immigrants give as much as they receive, and this not only by their work contribution to their new country in jobs and professions and services without which the economy of Western countries could not any more subsist, but also by their culture and character and traditions and outlook on life which contribute to enlighten, broaden, enrich the mentality of individuals and the shaping of society. It is important that the immigrants themselves become conscious of this. They are clearly aware of the value of their presence and their work for the countries that need their services, but they don't often realise that their presence among the old societies of the West is all the more valuable as a living witness to contrast in beliefs, alternatives in attitudes, openness towards different ways of life, and receptiveness of new understandings of the world. It is not only through the work of their hands and the exerting of their minds that immigrants benefit their adoptive country, but also and much more through their being different and their feeling diverse, through their otherness and their newness. As the shades of their colours and the variety of their smiles bring brightness and diversity to streets and offices, so the turn of their thought, the background of their reactions, the expressions of their idiom, the feasts of their calendar, the rites of their religion bring also colour and life to an old society, and that at a far deeper and more effective level than the mere contribution of manual or intellectual labour. Immigrants contribute culturally to the development of their new country as much as they receive from it, and this should be explicitly acknowledged by both sides. "In the integration between the two cultures the key word is reciprocity." (Maalouf).

International cuisine in the old world would not prosper if it were to stick to its own recipes and ignore dishes from remote kitchens around the world, but, on the contrary, it does revive jaded palates and enliven old menus by eastern dishes being recognised, accepted, and made popular, and then cooked as prescribed in each place of origin with old recipes and traditional kitchenware. The culinary panorama of the West would be much poorer without restaurants with names like "Taj", "Ganges", "Tandoori Palace", or "Mumbai Masala". Gastronomy is a vital part of culture, and a reminder, as we glance at the menu of *curries* and *biryanis* in any of the many popular Indian restaurants anywhere in Europe or America in anticipation of an exotic feast, that what the pungent dishes of Oriental cuisine do for our taste, the spicy ideas of Oriental mentality can do to our minds.

This means, as I keep insisting throughout the book, that immigrants must be conscious of their own identity and diversity, and must not blindly rush to embrace the ways of the people now around them, forgetting their own. The desire to be accepted, as we have seen, leads particularly second-generation immigrant youths to try to mix, to assimilate, to blend, to melt into the new society around them by entirely becoming, in mind as in dress and as fast as possible, like the people they live with. This effort is as well-meant as it is misdirected. The right way, once more, lies through the acceptance of both identities, never through the rejection of any of the two. Professional experts in the field reinforce the point: immigrants who try to merge too fast with their surroundings at the expense of their own customs and traditions don't do so well in work and in life as those who remain attached to the ways of their origin while they explore the new. It is those that learn to maintain and develop the double attachment that succeed better in their personal growth as well as in their social and professional life.

John Berry, Queen's University psychology Professor Emeritus and lead author of the largest ever international study of immigrant youth featuring 5,000 interviews in 13 countries along 10 years, has made a point which almost unexpectedly confirms the thesis of this book that the way to growth does not lie in uniformity but in diversity. He calls his own findings "a big surprise" to himself, and sets them out in clear conclusions:

> "Immigrant youth are better able to handle discrimination, have fewer emotional problems, and get along better in school and in the community when they remain strongly attached to their own ethnic culture rather than try to melt into a national culture. They do even better when they have a double attachment to both the national society and to their heritage culture.
>
> The big surprise here is that youth don't do so well either psychologically or socially if they try to

assimilate. Immigrants who try to assimilate from the start have poorer self-esteem, do not do as well in school, and exhibit more anti-social behaviour that those who integrate. Adolescents who are confident in their own ethnicity and proud of their ethnic group may be better able to deal constructively with discrimination, for example, by regarding it as the problem of the perpetrator or by taking proactive steps to combat it. Immigrant youth fare better in countries that have a strategy of promoting diversity than they do in countries that do not specifically support diversity." *(Escuela de Verano sobre Migraciones,* Valencia 2006, Document 9, p. 1)

"Assimilation" here is identification with the new culture forgoing the original one, while "integration" means the combination of both. And we are told that the keeping of both is a better way to health and success than the plunging into one. The haste we observed in the cases of some second-generation immigrants to forget background, heritage, language, colour, allegiances in order to be immediately accepted into the crowd without any differences or discrimination is counterproductive, as the aim is not usually achieved and frustration ensues.

"The secret dream of most migrants is to be taken for 'natives'. Their first temptation is to imitate their hosts, and sometimes they succeed in doing so. But more often they fail. They haven't got the right accent, the right shade of skin, the right first name, the right family name or the proper papers, so they are soon found out. A lot of them know it's no use even trying, and out of pride or bravado make themselves out to be more different than they really are. And needless to say some go even further, and their frustration turns into violent contestation." (Maalouf, p. 38)

Always the same situation. Any of the two extremes taken with the exclusion of the other leads to trouble. Total closeness and total distance are equally baleful. It is the balanced, conscious, delicate, respectful, tentatively undertaken and progressively obtained blending of the two cultures that gives the best results in personal growth and in social welfare. I am one and I am many, and the gradual realisation of my own developing and broadening identity is my real passport to happiness and fulfilment.

Thus we have come back, at the end of the book, to the fundamental question we asked at the beginning, Who am I? That is the basic issue of the immigration problem. Everything depends on it, and my inward peace and fruitful activity will follow upon my self-understanding and conscious integration within myself. I am many things, even different nationalities, preferences, homes, traditions, feelings, tastes, languages, cultures. There are different aspects in a single personality, and the richness and the individuality of my own character are preserved by acknowledging all and forgetting none. These different aspects are not successive layers or concentric circles, an image that would lead to devalue some aspects of my life while exalting others, but they are rather like the many different facets of a bright diamond. Each one is valid in itself, each one has its own angle, its own reflection, its own time, its own colour, and together they make up the wonder and the joy of my earthly existence.

When I celebrated my 80th birthday, my friends, knowing my good relationship with Angels, presented me with a little Swarovski Crystal Angel that presides over my desk since then. His wings, his mantle, his sleeves, his transparent surfaces and delicate robes are polished in miniature triangles that catch and reflect the ray of light in all the colours of the rainbow in the humility of an ordinary crystal and the variety of its multifaceted art. The Angel changes shades on its own, responds to every movement and presents a new light at every turn. I do not choose the colours of my Angel or prefer any of them to any other, but I admire them all, I enjoy his beauty and feel his company. I love my Angel.

Multifaceted is the word I want. It is what we are. Diamonds in the shaping. Many facets that reflect many lights and many events and many experiences and many memories. This does not mean that all the facets have to be shining at the same time. This would be as impossible as it would be awkward, and would spoil the work of art. But, on the other hand, this does mean that we cannot forget or suppress or ignore any facet, as the loss of a single facet entails the impoverishing of them all. Each facet comes to the fore at its own moment and under its own light. Thus I can feel an aspect of my personality in one occasion, and another in another. No contradiction. Simply asserting what I am at the moment, and never forgetting what I am on the whole.

I began the book with an anecdote, and will approach now its end with another. It is an anecdote which can be well understood both in England and in India, and which, in its sporting humour, can be a good illustration of the more complex problem of contrary feelings in the same heart. Although the depth and reach of the experience can only be appreciated by the consecrated followers of *the* game. A British friend of mine in India, great fan of cricket, a game which, together with the habit of drinking tea and the use of the English language, is the acknowledged and treasured heritage India received and has kept from Britain, told me once about the repeated conflict he experienced within himself every time India played England in cricket. Which side am I on? Which team do I want to win the match, the one of my native England or the one of my adopted India? What can I tell to people who ask me, who listen to the score with me, who watch me watch the game on television? How do I react when the English captain bowls a maiden over or when the Indian skipper is caught LBW? When do I clap and shout and jump and fire rockets at the end, when India wins or when England wins? (Ignoring, of course, for the moment, the appeasing fact that most five-day cricket test matches end up in a draw.) My friend had an answer ready, and it was a genuine one and an enlightening one, not just a clever dodge to escape an awkward situation. He used to say that if he was in India when the match was being played (wherever it was played in the international tournament), he would prefer England to win, in order to show his Indian friends how good English players were; while, if he was in England when the match was being played, he clearly and definitely wanted by all means India to win so as to show his English friends how good India was. British and Indian. One facet at a time. Both perfectly understandable. No contradiction, no friction, no opposition. Only allowing to shine at each moment the facet that faces the light. That is cricket.

We are many things, many faces, many persons in one, and we treasure them all. We have already a long personal history behind us, and we recognise it and allow each aspect of our personality to surface at the moment it is called for, we play the figure-ground Gestalt game letting one profile define itself at its time before its background only to fade again and yield to the new outline at the next contact with a new background with the flow of life, we embrace all that we are and have been and will be, we can

NEVER THE TWAIN

Rudyard Kipling's opening line in *The Ballad of East and West* is repeatedly on the lips of those who love both East and West, long for their embrace, and grieve over their estrangement:

"East is East, and West is West, and never the twain shall meet!"

"Never the twain." Decisive words. But the quotation is unfair. One should at least quote the first four lines in full:

"Oh, East is East, and West is West, and never the twain shall meet,
Till Earth and Sky stand presently at God's great Judgment Seat;
But there is neither East nor West, Border, nor Breed, nor Birth
When two strong men stand face to face tho' they come from the ends of the earth!"

Two strong men. Kamal is the Afghan chieftain who has stolen "the Colonel's mare that is the Colonel's pride". The son of the British colonel mounts his dun (horse with a black main) in pursuit of the rebel through The Tongue of Jagai. He fires his pistol at his enemy at full gallop, misses, trips on his dun and lies under it at the mercy of the Afghan chief. But Kamal will not strike a fallen foe.

"They have ridden the low moon out of the sky, their hoofs drum up the dawn,
The dun he went like a wounded bull, but the mare like a new-roused fawn.
The dun he fell at a water-course – in a woeful heap fell he,
And Kamal has turned the red mare back, and pulled the rider free.
He has knocked the pistol out of his hand – small room was there to strive,
'T'was only by favour of mine', quoth he, 'ye rode so long alive:
There was not a rock for twenty mile, there was not a clump of tree,
But covered a man of my own men with his rifle cocked on his knee.
If I had raised my bridle-hand, as I have held it low,
The little jackals that flee so fast, were feasting all in a row:
If I had bowed my head on my breast, as I have held it high,
The kite that whistles above us now were gorged till she could not fly.'

Lightly answered the Colonel's son: 'I hold by the blood of my clan:
Take up the mare for my father's gift – by God, she has carried a man!'
The red mare ran to the Colonel's son, and nuzzled against his breast,

'We be two strongmen', said Kamal then, 'but she loveth the younger best.

So she shall go with a lifter's dower, my turquoise-studded rein,
My broidered saddle and saddle-cloth and silver stirrups twain.'
The Colonel's son a pistol drew and held it muzzle-end,
'Ye have taken the one from a foe'. Said he; will ye take the mate from a friend?'
'A gift for a gift', said Kamal straight; 'a limb for the risk of a limb.
Thy father has sent his son to me, I'll send my son to him!'
With that he whistled his only son, that dropped from a mountain-crest,
He trod the grass like a buck in spring, and he looked like a lance in rest.
'Now here is thy master', Kamal said, 'who leads a troop of the Guides,
And thou must ride at his left side as shield on shoulder rides.
Till Death or I cut loose the tie, at camp and board and bed,
Thy life is his – thy fate it is to guard him with thy head.'

They have looked each other between the eyes, and there they found no fault,
They have taken the Oath of the Brother-in-Blood on leavened bread and salt:
They have taken the Oath of the Brother-in-Blood on fire and fresh-cut sod,
On the hilt and the haft of the Khyber knife, and the Wondrous Names of God."

I cannot read those lines without my eyes going wet.
Generosity, adventure, dignity, courage, encounter, trust.

Poetry and beauty. Touching revelation in verse of the deepest nobility in life. We, too, have now looked each other between the eyes, and there we find no fault. And we have been able to look straight because we now feel strong. Let us take the Oath of the Brother-in-Blood with all those we meet, we greet, we love, we fear, we trust, we mistrust, we understand, we misunderstand, we flee, we embrace. We are all brothers and sisters because we all feel now firm in our convictions, clear in our mind, open in our vision, strong in our heart.

"But there is neither East nor West, Border, nor Breed, nor Birth When two strong men stand face to face tho' they come from the ends of the earth!"